# FEILDEN CLEGG BRADLEY STUDIOS EDUCATION ARCHITECTURE URBANISM THREE UNIVERSITY PROJECTS

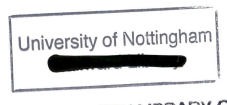

Artifice
books on architecture

# FEILDEN CLEGG BRADLEY STUDIOS EDUCATION ARCHITECTURE URBANISM THREE UNIVERSITY PROJECTS

# CONTENTS

1007360227

# JEREMY TILL
# THE THREE-
# LEGGED STOOL

30 years ago, the landscape of Higher Education in the United Kingdom was relatively stable: universities were given quotas for reasonable numbers of students, given money to construct buildings to house them in, and then more or less left to get on with it, and subject to only minimal scrutiny. Now, catalysed by the Thatcherite revolution, which ushered in the dominance of neo-liberal values, we are in a very different place. First, and most obviously, the UK university sector has expanded massively, with the numbers of students growing fivefold from around 0.5m in 1980 to nearly 2.5m now. Secondly, the 2011 White Paper introduced a whole series of measures that open up to the effective privatisation of higher education in the future. Behind the headlines of tripled fees (which in fact save the taxpayer no money because we still have to cover the cost of the student loans) other ideologically driven policies allow elite universities to expand as much as they want, play to the hands of the for-profit privateers, and introduce market-led principles to a system that has traditionally been based on the values of civic worth. Thirdly, and probably rightly, universities are subjected to increasing scrutiny through league tables, quality assurance checks and the publication of ever more data to inform student choice. Thus a threefold shift has been instigated—in numbers, in funding, in quality control.

These three key issues obviously impact on architecture, in perhaps conflicting manners. Although their genesis is particular to the UK, the effects have international resonances. The increase in numbers clearly results in more buildings but, more importantly, turns the traditionally inward-looking profile of the Medieval university inside-out. In UK cities like Sheffield, Leeds and Manchester the student population accounts for over ten per cent of the overall urban population, and the knowledge industry of the universities has now, as the largest local employers, replaced the manufacturing industries on which the cities were founded. Universities have thus become major players in the social and economic life of UK cities, and yet their architecture has only just started to respond to this civic responsibility. FCBS' Worcester building is a rare and inspiring example of educational and civic facilities merging spatially and sets an interesting new direction for others to follow. In other universities, for example Northumbria or Sunderland, there are successful contributions to the public realm, but generally university buildings are protected behind barriers, sending out mixed spatial messages about the public engagement of the knowledge industry and the role it might play in civic life.

Secondly, the introduction of market values in the UK and beyond, has meant that universities everywhere have had to become much more canny about positioning themselves in the global educational market. Buildings have become a prominent part of that profiling: a cursory flick through university websites and brochures shows new architecture featuring large. The word 'iconic' even pops up from time to time. The tower of FCBS' Leeds building is all over Leeds Metropolitan's publicity material, and quite rightly because it is a fine example of how architecture can be used to provide both spatial and corporate identity.

The third way that university architecture is having to respond to new conditions is in being responsive to student demand. Despite resistance from most academics, the notion of student as customer is now embedded in university parlance. The mantra of improving the student experience is endlessly played, with the volume to be turned ever higher when the new fees come in. League tables, government information sets, word-of-mouth—all these and more measure and disseminate the quality of that experience, and universities ignore the provision of that experience at their peril. Again architecture plays a prominent role, with a clear shift in priorities from the mere upgrading of traditional teaching accommodation to the provision of student focused spaces, often designated as social learning, or even just social spaces. Hybrid spatial programmes are evolving in which the new technologies of learning and the patterns of contemporary student life create as yet unheard-of spaces (hence the gawky naming of them as Hubs, Exchanges, Commons or whatever). FCBS' Manchester building is a good example of this emerging (non) typology, a place where boundaries of use and vision are purposely blurred.

What is interesting is how these three architectural demands—let us call them the civic, the iconic and the social—are often in competition, even in conflict, with each other. Thus the image-driven moment of the iconic instant does not necessarily sit comfortably with the looser, temporally-evolving, demands of the social. And accommodating the experience of students' social life is often done best away from the public responsibility of the civic. And the stridency of the iconic is usually incompatible with the soft life of the civic; ask any citizen of Dubai. The evolving university scene in the UK and beyond thus sets up a three-legged stool for architects to straddle and design for. It is a sometimes uneasy set of demands, and one that is always in motion as the competing parts push and pull for space; in the end a three-legged stool will settle to some stability, but some will be more unsettling to view and engage with than others. The three projects in the book show FCBS facing up to these potential instabilities in a fleet-footed and non-dogmatic manner, and one which has the added advantage of touching the earth as lightly as architecture can. My hunch, however, is that the real legacy of the book lies not in the individual projects, but in the way that lessons from them might be developed to show us all how the three-legged stool might evolve and be spatialised in the future.

# JOHN BROOKS INTRODUCTION

It is hard to over-emphasise the changes that are happening to Higher Education in England due to the effective withdrawal of public funding and the full cost of their education being paid by future graduates through personal taxation. More than ever before this places students at the centre of Higher Education, and their experience of all aspects of our educational service becomes critical.

The end of capital funding for teaching means that universities must make their own commercial and educational judgements about investing in new infrastructure. This judgement will be strongly influenced by market position, student demand, condition and location of existing buildings and operational effectiveness. The 'free market' in Higher Education, with increased and diversified choice and more relevant information, encourages students to make their personal investment decisions wisely.

Universities must exploit the opportunities offered by the free market, and should not lament the loss of public funding as it is clear that this will never return. The challenges are significant and yet the freedom to determine your market position, to generate income and to make appropriate long-term investment will ultimately further strengthen strong institutions. Other freedoms come from the availability of new technology to radically transform our thinking about the learning environment and, centrally, the relationship between teacher and learner and the behaviour of new communities of learners. All of these opportunities liberate universities to transform their approach to teaching, learning, student experience and to invest in new buildings truly fit for the twenty-first century.

Another significant challenge is to ensure long-term environmental sustainability—which in reality goes well beyond the BREEAM score! Here the opportunity is to embrace new designs which enable us to reduce our dependency on energy and water, and to reduce the waste that we create. This agenda is about both building design, and how the building is used. Environmental culture must become all pervasive within the organisation. For universities, students are quite often the best ambassadors for 'green' behaviour and buildings. Universities have a responsibility to embed environmental issues into the curriculum and learning, and to take a leading role in exploiting innovation in environmental design and technology. The Holy Grail of the Three Zeros Campus—zero energy, zero water and zero waste—is within our grasp. The combination of these three factors:
- the free market and informed student choice
- innovation in learning technology
- environmental sustainability

creates a new dynamic for the specification and design of new academic buildings. In addition, universities have an increasingly important civic or community function. They provide powerful visual symbols for investment in the future and embody the ambitions and aspirations of future generations. Many stand for widening participation and community engagement, while others symbolise scientific advancement and economic development. All universities are crucial elements in developing strong communities and economic vitality. It is therefore important that, as well as delivering functional excellence, our buildings make strong and unambiguous external statements about the role, purpose and position of the university.

The most important part of the design process is the dialogue between the end user and the architect, and in particular the initial 'word picture' describing the ambition

and purpose of the building. To this end it is essential that the university establishes effective internal discussion groups to build up a detailed description of use, establishes external consultation groups to engage fully and, at an early stage, with their community and civic partners; and identifies a single point of contact with the architectural design team to maintain unambiguous communication. Time spent discussing and consulting is a sound investment in future success!

The importance of communication and the development of a shared vision between the city and the university is well illustrated in our experience in the design of the Manchester Metropolitan University (MMU) Business School and Student Hub. MMU operates a large and comprehensive Business School of some 5,000 students, and the Hub will become the information and administration home for our 30,000 Manchester-based students. There are two effective 'users' of the building: the Business School and Student and Academic Services. The lead user role was given to the Dean of the Business School, and initial sums indicated a 25,000 square metre building with a budget of £75 million. The proposed site was on the main campus adjacent to the Mancunian Way (an elevated motorway), approximately one kilometre from the city centre and forming an important gateway into the City and the Education Corridor. Because of the prominence of the location and the important statement the building would make about University-City partnerships, a design competition was chaired by the Leader of the City Council, Sir Richard Leese. The selection panel was unanimous in selecting the concept proposed by Keith Bradley of Feilden Clegg Bradley Studios. Today, as we start to occupy and use the building, there is a remarkable correlation between the original design concept and the actual building.

The design concept started from the vision of learning being a social activity, achieved within a variety of different environments from the formal to the informal and from the organised to the chaotic. The high level objective was the exchange of knowledge. Manchester is renowned for its 'Exchange' buildings where the original industrial city exchanged goods and services. These buildings were characterised by functional spaces surrounding large open spaces where natural light and the grandeur of the space created a conducive business exchange environment. This became the masterplan for our new building—the exchange building for the twenty-first century would exchange business knowledge and understanding. Detailed planning determined the mix of lecture theatres, seminar rooms and office accommodation—but the difficult part was to try and quantify how much flexible, open social learning space to provide and how this would be configured. The simplicity of the design—three unequal height towers rising within an enclosed glass envelope—gave considerable flexibility, with two large atria becoming the centre pieces for the Hub and social learning. A fundamental decision was to express high quality by the use of materials with a very limited palette of fair-faced concrete and glass. This would help to achieve excellent environmental qualities using the exposed thermal mass of the building and cool slab technology to maintain a base temperature. The roofs were sloping and south-facing providing the ideal conditions for the PV arrays which covered all the solid elements. In addition the atria provided natural thermal uplift and hence air circulation.

The external appearance also echoed the fundamental simplicity of the design, the environmental qualities and the open aspect of learning contained within. Uniquely the envelope was visualised as a skirt with pleats which folded and enclosed the building. The pleats were expressed as glazed fins with photo chromic interference films which reflected and refracted vertical bands of light into and from the building.

This has given the building as a whole stunning optical properties: different colours of the spectrum refract into the atria and reflect from the external walls. The colour and intensity of the vertical beams of light alter with the angle of incidence of the sun's rays creating a dynamic spectral response. The combination of stunning design and optical intrigue has created a gateway building into the university campus.

In summary, the project has progressed smoothly from conceptualisation to delivery. Large university developments, particularly those with strong city links, have become important civic facilities and part of the public domain. With increasing fees and a desire to continue to increase participation and to accommodate diversity it is important that modern university buildings make clear and unambiguous statements about world class facilities and access to learning.

The design process critically depends upon an effective partnership between user and designer, and then with the builder. The interaction is not simple and requires all concerned to learn a common language. The most effective discussions are truly interactive and two-way, and both sides of the partnership must feel able to challenge and to be challenged. Higher Education is evolving new approaches to learning spaces and staff accommodation, and architectural practices have broad and diverse experience of other commercial and professional worlds to bring to the design table. Most importantly, constrained budgets do not mean poor quality buildings, they quite simply place even greater demand on high quality design and on freezing the design, thus avoiding costly in process design changes.

Has the project been a success? I believe so. Will we learn more as the building becomes fully operational? Of course it will be for future generations of users—we estimate more than one million students over the building's lifetime—to judge if this beautiful, innovative and inspiring building stands the test of time.

# ANDREW HARRISON
# THE CHANGING
# LEARNING LANDSCAPE

Rethinking the university is necessary in the light of the monumental changes that are taking place in society. These include the impacts of globalisation, the proliferation of information technology, including the Internet, changing demographics of the learning population, changes in government policies, including fee structures for students, and the support of research and teaching in publicly funded institutions.

In addition student expectations about the learning experience are changing (student as customer, student as producer) and the blurring of learning, living, working and leisure within many people's lives is having a huge impact. From an institutional point of view resources are becoming increasingly scarce and many universities are facing increased competition and pressures in a global educational market where students can choose where, how and when they want to learn.

British universities have been guilty of a failure to redefine their identity in a new, diverse world of Higher Education.... The most essential task is to recreate a sense of our own work by refashioning our understanding of our identity—our understanding of what the word 'university' means."[1]

Approaches to learning in educational settings are changing. Traditional teacher-centred models, where good teaching is conceptualised as the passing on of sound academic, practical or vocational knowledge, are being replaced with more student-centred approaches which emphasise the construction of knowledge through shared situations.

Barr and Tagg suggest that this shift from an "instruction paradigm" to a "learning paradigm" has changed the role of the higher and further education institution from "a place of instruction" to "a place to produce learning".[2] This is partly driven by changing educational requirements. The shift to a knowledge driven economy is driving demand for a more qualified, highly skilled, creative and flexible workforce. There is less emphasis on factual knowledge, and more on the ability to think critically and solve complex problems. Knowles argues that, in the modern world, the most socially useful thing to learn is the process of learning.[3]

The increasing diversity of student populations has prompted a new, more tailored, approach to learning. The shift towards student-centred teaching modes has been supported by a growing body of research and theory, pointing to the benefits of a range of learning styles and individual preferences. The factors influencing how we learn include changes in learning style, the impact of a wide range of technologies that can support learning and teaching and a variety of integrating forces including 'on the job' workplace-based learning, increased interdisciplinary learning in schools, further and higher education and technology convergence which has created multipurpose devices supporting learning, leisure and working.

The shift in learning paradigm has direct implications for the university estate. Traditional categories of space are becoming less meaningful as space becomes less specialised, boundaries blur, and operating hours extend toward 24/7. In many institutions space types are increasingly being designed primarily around patterns of human interaction rather than specific needs of particular departments, disciplines or technologies.

*learning landscape*
*catagories learning spaces*
*{ specialist*
*{ general*
*{ informal*

*Are you sure?*

New space models for universities may focus as much on enhancing quality of life as they do on directly supporting the learning experience. The 'learning landscape' concept has been used to develop spatial models for universities that recognise that learning is not just confined to formal teaching spaces and that the quality of the student experience is impacted by all aspects of their physical environment. Learning spaces within this model can be categorised as 'specialist', 'general' or 'informal';

- Specialised Learning Spaces, tailored to specific functions or teaching approaches
- Generic Learning Spaces adaptable for multiple uses and teaching approaches and
- Informal Learning Spaces that support ad hoc, individuals and small groups.[4]

Many institutions are seeking to minimise the amount of specialised learning space and to instead create highly adaptable teaching and learning spaces that can be shared across faculties and subject areas.

In her ground-breaking 2006 book *Learning Spaces*, Diana Oblinger, now Director of Educause, noted that today's students—whether 18, 22, or 55—have attitudes, expectations and constraints that differ from those of students even ten years ago. She suggests that learning spaces often reflect the people and learning approach of the times, so spaces designed in 1956 are not likely to fit perfectly with students today.

> Learning is the central activity of colleges and universities. Sometimes that learning occurs in classrooms (formal learning); other times it results from serendipitous interactions among individuals (informal learning). Space—whether physical or virtual—can have an impact on learning. It can bring people together; it can encourage exploration, collaboration, and discussion. Or, space can carry an unspoken message of silence and disconnectedness. More and more we see the power of built pedagogy (the ability of space to define how one teaches).[5]

Many of today's learners favour active, participatory, experiential learning—the learning style they exhibit in their personal lives. But their behaviour may not match their self-expressed learning preferences when sitting in a large lecture hall with chairs bolted to the floor. The single focal point at the front of the room sends a strong signal about how learning will occur.

Information technology has also fundamentally changed how we learn. Collecting, analysing, displaying, and disseminating knowledge typically involves IT. Retrieving information has become an IT function; students often consider the Internet, not the library, their information universe. Rather than trying to know everything, students and faculty increasingly rely on networks of peers and databases of information. Oblinger also states that increased understanding about how people learn has also changed our ideas about learning space.

> There is value from bumping into someone and having a casual conversation. There is value from hands-on, active learning as well as from discussion and reflection. There is value in being able to receive immediate support when needed and from being able to integrate multiple activities (such as writing, searching, and computing) to complete a project. And, there is value from learning that occurs in authentic settings, such as an estuary or on a trading floor. How do we turn the entire campus—and many places off campus—into an integrated learning environment?

As we have come to understand more about learners, how people learn, and technology, our notions of effective learning spaces have changed. Increasingly, those spaces are flexible and networked; bringing together formal and informal activities in a seamless environment that acknowledges that learning can occur anyplace, at any time, in either physical or virtual spaces.[6]

Also in 2006 the JISC publication *Designing Spaces for Effective Learning: A guide to 21st century learning space design* noted that an educational building is an expensive long-term resource. As a consequence the design of its individual spaces needs to be:

- Flexible—to accommodate both current and evolving pedagogies
- Future-proofed—to enable space to be re-allocated and reconfigured
- Bold—to look beyond tried and tested technologies and pedagogies
- Creative—to energise and inspire learners and tutors
- Supportive—to develop the potential of all learners
- Enterprising—to make each space capable of supporting different purposes.

"A learning space should be able to motivate learners and promote learning as an activity, support collaborative as well as formal practice, provide a personalised and inclusive environment, and be flexible in the face of changing needs."[7]

Traditional categories of space on campus will become less meaningful as space becomes less specialised, boundaries blur, and operating hours extend toward 24/7.

Space types will be designed primarily around patterns of human interaction rather than specific needs of particular departments, disciplines or technologies and new space models will focus on enhancing quality of life as much as on supporting the direct learning experience.[8]

If these transformations happen the campus will continue to be relevant and a core part of future generations' learning experiences, albeit supported by a wide range of other physical and virtual spaces and learning experiences. The university of the future will be inclusive of broad swaths of the population, actively engaged in issues that concern them and relatively open to commercial influence.[9]

As Temple stated in his 2007 literature review of *Learning Spaces for the 21st century*:

> Taking a broad sweep of nearly a thousand years of university construction, it is possible to draw one significant conclusion. Of all building types none more conspicuously links new ideals of design and innovative technologies to the mission of development than the university. The exacting agendas of intellectual inquiry, of scientific experiment and refined taste are historically to be found in the design of many university buildings. For example, the sense of scientific rationalism is embodied in built form in the ancient universities of Oxford, Cambridge, Paris, Bologna and Turin. The ideals of democracy find expression in the layout of universities from Virginia to Cape Town... the campus has never been an ordinary place.[10]

The current threats and challenges to higher education were highlighted by Den Heijer in 2011, particularly in a Dutch context but applying internationally. In particular she cited problems emerging from an ageing and poorly maintained educational estate, the impact of rapidly increasing student numbers—an increase from about

100 million to 200 million students by 2025. She states that the future university campus will have to be flexible enough to accommodate a population that is less predictable in size and more diverse in character and notes the "importance of the campus for the university's performance—positively or negatively influencing production, attractiveness and competiveness in an international market for knowledge workers —is confirmed by networks of campus managers all over the world, by rapidly growing universities as well as universities that struggle with decline or quality issues."[11]

## Specialised Learning Spaces

**Tailored to specific functions or teaching modalities**

**Limited setting types:**
formal teaching, generally enclosed

**Access:**
Embedded, departmental

**Tend to be:**
- owned within departments, subject specific
- involve specialised equipment
- require higher levels of performance specification
- often higher security concerns

## Generic Learning Spaces

**Range of classroom types**

**Range of setting types:**
formal teaching, open and enclosed

**Access:**
In general circulation zones, access by schedule

**Tend to be:**
- generic teaching settings
- often limited in flexibility
- by furnishings
- used when scheduled

## Informal Learning Spaces

**Broad definition of learning space**

**Wide range of setting types:**
informal and formal, social, open and enclosed

**Access:**
Public, visible, distributed, inclusive

**Tend to:**
- encompass richer range of settings
- allow choice
- be loose fit, unscheduled
- work as a network of spaces rather
- than singular settings
- have food!

Source: DEGW/Andrew Harrison

The learning experience will become increasingly multi-layered with learning spaces providing a number of flexible activity zones to support learning, living and working. Users will be able to choose appropriate settings and technology for the tasks they want to achieve. The spaces and experiences will change over the course of the day, changing to reflect different types of users at different times of the day. More space will be devoted to collaborative activities, and informal meeting and work areas will need to be provided to support mobile learners.

There will be a requirement for ergonomic, easily reconfigurable furniture and power everywhere in the short to mid-term at least. In the longer term the performance of laptop batteries is likely to improve to the point where a full day's use will be possible with a single charge or through the use of hydrogen fuel cells for laptops.

Learning spaces will need to be able to incorporate a wide range of technology-enabled work settings able to support larger or multiple screens, webcams, tele-presence systems, voice input and increased use of audio/video materials. In 2004 William Mitchell from MIT stated that the forms and functions of learning spaces were changing rapidly as architects discovered new ways to take advantage of computer and communications technologies. He believed that as the new types of learning space were incorporating new technologies they were also creating new patterns of social and intellectual interaction, altering the demand for space on campus and suggesting new strategies of overall campus design: "The entire campus becomes an interactive learning device."[12]

He felt that all campus space, including outdoor spaces and mobile spaces, should be considered as potentially wirelessly serviced ad-hoc classrooms. The impact of information technology on learning spaces was further discussed by Diana Oblinger in 2004 in her article "Leading the Transition from Classrooms to Learning Spaces", published by Educause in 2005.

> The Internet has changed notions of place, time, and space. Space is no longer just physical; it incorporates the virtual. New methods of teaching and learning, based on an improved understanding of cognition, have emerged, as well. As a result, the notion of a classroom has expanded and evolved; the space need no longer be defined by 'the class' but by 'learning'.[13]

Acker and Miller (2005) noted that new learning space design paradigms must adapt to student learning styles while still taking account of the institution's need for fiscal efficiencies: "Previously, the cost savings associated with large lecture halls, fixed seating and minimal investments in technology drove decision-making. Today, the emphasis is more balanced, and the roles that attractive learning spaces play in bringing the most accomplished students and faculty to campus and in increasing student engagement with learning are better recognised."[14]

The importance of considering the whole campus as a learning environment was also stressed by Jamieson (2009) in his article "The Serious Matter of Informal Learning". He suggests that the future university will need to consist of a mix of formal classroom types, with traditional-style spaces for more didactic, larger classes and new-generation spaces for more collaborative, active learning approaches.[15]

He believed that many universities regard the provision of informal learning spaces as a less serious matter than the requirements for formal teaching spaces and consequently they committed less resource to these spaces. Jamieson defines informal learning as those "other" activities students do to learn between formal classes, including course reading, class preparation, and assignments and project activity. He notes that learning involves social interaction and it is not easy to separate purely student social activity from that which is learning-related, particularly as both forms of peer-to-peer engagement often take place in the same campus settings and states that informal learning typically takes place in the library, the student refectory, cafes, and other social spaces.[16]

While historically the university campus has been shaped by the emphasis on traditional instructional methods and the classrooms this has required, Jamieson believes that the future campus will be determined to a large extent by the university's response to informal learning with the balance of formal and informal settings changing as students are required to be more self-directed.

Social hubs are appearing as key features of campus life, along with internal 'student streets' within buildings that feature a mix of functions expected to promote both social and learning-related activity. Jamieson states that another institutional response has been the creation of comprehensive student centres that offer key administrative and course support along with information technology access and other services.[17]

It is also important to recognise that learning activity extends well beyond the edges of the campus, both physically as well as virtually. Recognition of community-based learning spaces may be limited to off campus access to virtual learning environments or may extend to semi-programmed use of public space for small group study or discussion.

While campuses may evolve slowly as new land is acquired or buildings replaced or renovated, the cycle of change is accelerating rapidly at the level of the spaces within the campus. Innovation is not just occurring in formal and learning settings on campus. As can be seen in the table on page 15, virtually every space type on campus is being radically rethought to see how the student and staff experience can be improved and the efficiency and effectiveness of every square metre of space on campus enhanced.

1. Graham, G, *Universities: The Recovery of an Idea*, Thorverton: Imprint Academic, 2002, p. 119.
2. Barr and Tagg 1995. *From teaching to learning: A new paradigm for undergraduate education*. http://ilte.ius.edu/pdf/barrtagg.pdf.
3. Knowles, MS, et al, *The Adult Learner: The definitive classic in adult education and human resource development*, Butterworth-Heinemann, 2011.
4. Dugdale, S, and P Long, *Planning the informal learning landscape*, ELI webinar, 12 March 2007.
5. Oblinger, D, *Learning Spaces*, Educause, 2006, Section 1.2.
6. Oblinger, D, *Learning Spaces*, Educause, 2006, Section 1.
7. JISC, *Designing Spaces for Effective Learning: A guide to 21st century learning space design*, HEFCE, 2006. p. 3. Downloaded from http://www.jisc.ac.uk/media/documents/publications/learningspaces.pdf.
8. DEGW, unpublished presentation, 2009.
9. Editorial. *Nature*. 446, 949 (26 April 2007).
10. Temple, P, *Learning Spaces for the 21st century*, London: Higher Education Academy,
2007 p. 27. Downloaded from http://www.heacademy.ac.uk/assets/documents/research/Learning_spaces_v3.pdf.
11. Den Heijer, A, *Managing the University Estate*, Delft: Eburon Academic Publishers, 2011, p. 34.
12. Mitchell, William J, "Rethinking Campus and Classroom Design", presentation at the NLII 2004 Fall Focus Session, 9 September 2004, Cambridge, MA, <http:// www.educause.edu/librarydetailpage/ 666&id=nli0438>.
13. Oblinger, *EDUCAUSE QUARTERLY* Number 1, 2005, p. 14.
14. Acker, SR, and MD Miller, *Campus Learning Spaces: Investing in How Students Learn*, Educause Center for Applied Research Research Bulletin, vol. 2005, issue 8, April 12, 2005, p. 2. http://net.educause.edu/ir/library/pdf/ERB0508.pdf.
15. Jamieson, Peter, "The Serious Matter of Informal Learning", *Planning for Higher Education*, 37(2), 2009, pp. 18–25.
16. Jamieson, "The Serious Matter of Informal Learning", p. 19.
17. Jamieson, "The Serious Matter of Informal Learning", p. 19.

# KEITH BRADLEY
# THE UNIVERSITY
# AND THE CITY

UNIVERSITY IN THE CITY

The city from a simple settlement became the place of the assembled institutions.
LOUIS KAHN

The city is an alchemy of endless different elements—societies, groups, races, religions—overlapping and interacting over time. Places generated from the geography of a place and a reason to exist—people drawn together for trade, pleasure, and occupation that have defined the progress of society, whether it be Venice in the sixteenth century or Manchester in the late nineteenth; they are the mark of each generation.

They are the epicentres of regions that celebrate the assembly and governance of their people—a vital city lifts the heart and stirs the blood of native and visitor and educates us in its contemporary values and those of our ancestors. The city teaches us about life in all its dimensions and the universal principles of people wanting to be together in districts or neighbourhoods for social, spiritual and material benefit—it's human nature! An education!

The university and the city have this symbiotic relationship that from its earliest historical roots has changed in a way that embraces this mutual reliance and an interdependency that is now an essential cultural and economic force. It is interesting to trace the genealogy of this relationship and how it has affected the context of the typological response to the form and nature of the modern university building.

> The snow had only just stopped, and in the court below my rooms all sounds were dulled. There were only a few sounds to hear, for it was early in January, and the college was empty and quiet; I could just make out the footsteps of the porter, as he passed beneath the window on his last round at night.
> ELLIOT IN HIS ROOMS, 1937, FROM CP SNOW'S *THE MASTERS*

Universities began as colleges in the twelfth to thirteenth century in Cambridge and Oxford. These early colleges were formed by clergymen in the churches or chapels for religious duties, using adjoining houses for teaching. The fourteenth century saw these translated into privately funded institutions for the ruling classes similar in general arrangement to the monastic establishments from which they came and based on the plan of the Medieval house, with a hall and rooms grouped around a quadrangle or

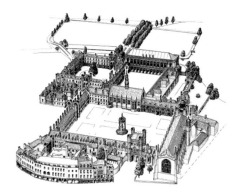

court. They were the origins of the fabric of these cities as they grew to serve the affluent masters and their students as the principle dominant force as an integral part of the life and governance of the place. A return to this integration and interdependence many generations later would arise in a different form based on egalitarian values to form the modern urban campus. Then, as now, the universities were a catalyst for growth.

> Every college and university is a urbanistic unit in itself, a town, small or large.
> LE CORBUSIER, 1937

After the World Wars it was a more enlightened Cambridge that led the way towards the modern university 'campus'. Walter Gropius was an *émigré* in Cambridge in the inter-war period and had made a modernist proposal for Christ's College which was rejected. However, this influenced the Casson Conder Sidgwick Avenue Plan for the Cambridge Arts Faculties prepared in 1952 and implemented in 1956. This was concurrent with Leslie Martin's appointment as the head of the Cambridge School of Architecture—Martin was from the LCC and brought with him a humanitarian Welfare State ethos of modern architecture from mainland Europe.

Whilst he started to influence the university and colleges with this new architecture, it was the advent of a new college project that was to be the most influential. The Churchill College Competition was launched in 1958 with Martin as one of the assessors and the shortlist would provide a who's who of the architects for the new generation of New Universities across the country. The finalists of Sheppard Robson (winners), Howell Killick Partridge, Chamberlain Powell Bon, Stirling Gowan and others like the young Smithsons produced bold and imaginative new models that would go on to influence the direction of modern university architecture and urbanism.

Universities became utopian models—idealised as microcosms of towns that would represent a more open diverse society. The Leeds University project by Chamberlain Powell Bon in 1960—which built into the fabric of the city with a high density set of courts linked by the new concept of pedestrian street decks—was the first to explore these concepts of connection and permeability of the new type of university city block.

These models were to be taken out of town inspired by new models in the US and Europe such as Candilis Josic Woods Free University on the outskirts of Berlin in 1963. The UK campuses of York, Bath, Sussex, Kent, Essex *et al* were to follow suit. Independent and self-contained Higher Education settlements, like the New Towns, were separated from the old, as suburbanisation and zoning took their foothold in planning for the next three decades.

> The modern city should be dense and many centred, a city of overlapping activity, an ecological city, a city of easy contact, an equitable city, and not least a beautiful city in which art, architecture and landscape can move to satisfy the human spirit.
> RICHARD ROGERS, 1995, REITH LECTURE AS REPORTED BY SIR CRISPIN TICKELL IN
> *CITIES FOR A SMALL PLANET*

The 1990s saw the start of the UK re-evaluating its cities and towns as part of what was then coined an Urban Renaissance. The zoning, separation and continuing sprawl of post-war Britain meant that the traditional vibrancy and intensity of the centre of our cities and towns was being degraded. Also the demise or removal of major industries from our urban centres left vast tracks of underused land, now known as 'brownfield' sites.

**top** Trinity College, Cambridge.

**bottom** Leeds University, Chamberlain, Powell and Bon.

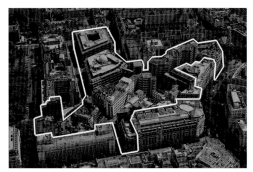

The 1995 Rogers Reith lectures captured a notion that our cities were becoming dysfunctional places as we focused on US-style zoning and car-orientated planning. The compact modern European city as exemplified by Paris, Amsterdam and, in contemporary extensions like the post-Olympic development of Barcelona, were setting models for the revival of the UK city. The publication of Rogers' seminal book *Cities for a Small Planet* coincided with the 1997 General Election and a new Labour government in power with an unprecedented majority, and coming into office with a rapidly improving economy. In 1998 the Deputy Prime Minister asked Richard Rogers to set up an urban task force to identify the causes of urban decline and formulate a vision for our cities based on the principles of design excellence, social well-being and environmental responsibility. "Towards an Urban Renaissance", a report produced in 1999, included a number of recommendations that informed central and local government policy followed by fiscal and legal frameworks.

By 2005 a follow up report reflected on the successes for regeneration with over 70 per cent of development on 'brownfield' land. Cities like Manchester were being transformed with a massive increase in the city centre populations with sustainable high density developments, with a huge investment in public transportation and public spaces. UK cities were again becoming the cultural, social and economic heartlands that could stand alongside our envied European neighbours at the start of a new millennium.

Universities were to play a major part in regeneration—the older established universities were complemented with the making of the new metropolitan and city universities from the polytechnics in the 1990s. With greater government investment, encouraged access to Higher Education, alongside the culture of focusing on city centres, a new generation of urban university estate plans was to be implemented. The expansion of the city university became a major economic force of physical and social regeneration. Outside London, cities like Manchester grew rapidly with around 100,000 students and staff in their universities.

> Instead of housing or working areas, it's important to create places for living —parts of towns where dwelling, work, study, and recreation take place in as close contact with one another as possible—equally important for an individual building as in a community plan.
> **RALPH ERSKINE ON DEMOCRATIC ARCHITECTURE**

Most worldwide cities have a 'knowledge city' programme where their universities have integrated urban campuses and are taking a central role in cultural, economic and social development. In contrast to the monocultural and greenfield campus of monolithic teaching and research facilities that separated civic structures and public life, these are clusters that reintegrate large scale institutions within the urban fabric and make an indigenous identity of place with a human scale—re-engaging with traditional urban spaces of streets and squares. In the UK the major nineteenth century-founded universities like the London University Colleges have grown incrementally around estate acquisition and a finer scale approach to new development of academic teaching, research and residential accommodation. The London School of Economics in Holborn is an extreme example—old and new buildings occupy a historic district of alleyways and small squares in subservience to the urban structure of organic shifts of improvised reuse and new stitching, creating a rich diversity of spaces inside and outside.

**top** Free University, Berlin.

**bottom** London School of Economics, Holborn.

> Make of each a place, a bunch of places of each house and each house a city, for a house is a tiny city, a city a huge house.
> **ALDO VAN EYCK**

Education is a social activity. Though technology gives us as individuals the ability to learn and acquire knowledge in new and previously impossible ways, every education institute is in a sense a society—socialising as a community experience of education.

The contemporary programme of the multi-functional polycentric city is replicated in the modern university estate. Integrated and contextually bespoke, each building responds to its setting as part of the city fabric. The boundaries between the institution and the life of the city is softened by interaction of use and a shared public realm. Academic staff and students are part of a more complex urban life, working and living outside the institution. Whether it be the professor who has commercial research partners and consultancy practice or the student who works part time in one of the neighbourhood restaurants, there is a substantial social overlap. The shared public spaces act as thresholds to the universities and the city the place of blurred boundaries and social interaction. A transition through either visual or physical permeability connects the institution's activities to its place and facilitates access to learning.

The metaphor of city living as model for learning translates into buildings that offer a sense of strong identity but non-deterministic forms—allowing a degree of occupation from the more informal lobbies, foyers and social spaces as the real 'classrooms' that then serve the more specific spaces of lecture theatres, seminar rooms, laboratories and studios. Internal thresholds and 'in-between' spaces of circulation, stairs and lift waiting spaces are planned to offer the opportunities of social and educational interaction. Contrasting as well as complimentary functions create adjacencies that become creative interfaces of disciplines. It is at these juxtapositions of spaces and activities that we see the advances of learning and research, again following the patterns that characterise the rich mix of a polycentric city.

> It is, in fact, nothing short of a miracle that the modern methods of instruction have not entirely strangled the holy curiosity of enquiry.
> ALBERT EINSTEIN

However flexible and accommodating of the vast range of activities within, these university buildings become recognisable cornerstones forming the highlights of our cities. If knowledge is power then their representation should underline that status as the new civic order. Corporations and dwellings should be the ordinary 'stuff' of our cities and the new universities the 'highlights' as civic buildings alongside the churches, museums, galleries and town halls. These buildings, as their civic partners, should be responsive to place with a strength of identity unique to its institution. We present in this book three unique buildings in three different cities, as examples of this thesis for an evolved university in the city: Broadcasting Place in Leeds, the Hive in Worcester, and the Hub in Manchester.

## BROADCASTING PLACE IN LEEDS—THE COURT AND THE TOWER

At the highest point of Leeds and adjacent to the inner ring road motorway, a court and tower building forms an edge perimeter and a marker for the Metropolitan University. A low cavorting terrace of academic teaching accommodation engages with the surrounding streets in alignment and scale to form a collegiate courtyard. These horizontal terraces then rise in a twisting mass of a tower accommodating student rooms that gestures back to the scattering of city centre landmarks.

top Manchester Metropolitan University Business School and Student Hub.

bottom Broadcasting Place, Leeds Metropolitan University.

The responsive form 'clasps' two listed nineteenth century buildings that represent an earlier generation of civic buildings—a Victorian Gothic church and neo-Greek

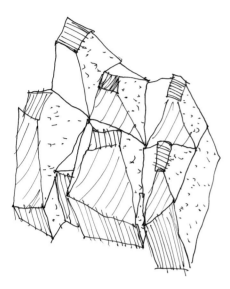

Classical early BBC building called Broadcasting House. The intertwining of the old and new creates human and super-scale spaces—contrasting forms representing that rich and contradictory mix of the contemporary city. The ensemble is held together by a distinctive skin of corten steel—a deep rust red relates to the sandstone of the adjoining terraces and surrounding geology. This strong physical identity culminating in its tower skyline captures a protected ground plane of public realm as a threshold to the institution. The general public, students and staff of the art school spaces mingle as they walk or linger in the court spaces with passages and vistas giving glimpses to the internal social, teaching and studio rooms. The entrances and elevations of the university command and interact with the space. Internally, the trailing terraces represent flexible and adaptable teaching and studio spaces that can be divided up in slices horizontally or vertically—the form is maintained and the interior adapts to the changing needs of the institution.

### THE HIVE IN WORCESTER—CITY ROOMS AND CONES

In the river valley adjacent to the ancient city walls of Worcester is poised a cluster of golden tiled cones—a crustacean on the edge of the floodplain that forms the new university and city library. Against the backdrop of the peaks and valleys of the Malvern Hills its articulated skyline of pyramidical roofs has the presence of a domed and minaretted second cathedral for the city—this one for the profane life of sharing facts and knowledge, rather than the sacred worship of an invisible god. The Hive is a collection of grand rooms that is a spiritually uplifting new generation library; the cones represent light filled containers of acquired knowledge. It connects with the city at an upper level bridge extension to the city wall walk and at a lower level with a new protected street court—the confluence of these routes bringing you into a dramatic entrance space on the city side. The lower levels of social library spaces then open out to the river view in the manner of an inside outside belvedere—a transparency and openness that announces the library to the city and its riverscape and *vice versa*.

The internal arrangement of volumes and spaces represents a miniaturised landscape —ravines and caverns, promontories and *plateaux* of floors linked by undulating stairs and landings that create informal learning spaces. These movement and interaction spaces lead to a 'hive' of interconnected rooms for individual or group study used by the general public and university students. This co-ownership of an internal space of the usually rarefied academic library is one of the most radical steps in the integration of the university and the city. The maturity of this approach is further extended as the building incorporates a one-stop-shop for city services, a children's library and city archive. A polycentric building that is indeed a peoples' palace of accessible civic rooms.

### THE HUB IN MANCHESTER—A LEARNING EXCHANGE

The MMU Business School and Student Hub building represents a 'lodged jewel' in an urban estate of incremental functional university buildings built across more than a century, disaggregated architecturally but held together by the public All Saints Garden Square. This significant public space is a rare green garden alcove off the north–south artery off Manchester's Oxford Road—the principle urban corridor that links the two universities with the commercial and cultural heart of the city. At this junction the raised section of the 'Mancunian' super highway flies across the historic urban grid and forms a twentieth century heroic edge to the MMU Hub site. Georgian garden square on one side, motorway on the other: the building form needs to resolve these two worlds both in plan and section.

**top** Broadcasting Place, context sketch.

**bottom** The Hive, concept sketch.

**opposite top** Manchester Metropolitan University Business School and Student Hub concept model.

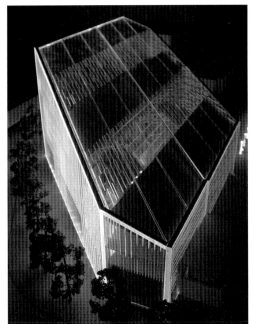

An urban hub as well as a hub of shared university functions that, from its kooky corner, needed to announce itself. The form is hewn as an irregular jewel of variegated glass, shaped to respond to a new pedestrian ante space off the square on the one side and the heroic scale of the super highway and the city centre on the other. A multifaceted building of inclined planes that are folded into a series of glass pleats that catch the light with reflection and refracted colour. A giant kaleidoscopic cloak that brightens up the generally overcast Manchester skyline and illuminates as decorative lampshade in the corner of the university square at night.

At ground level the upper dipping glass object form sits on a masonry plinth that follows the frontages and perimeter of the site, and opens into a covered colonnaded entrance off a smaller public threshold space leading from the garden square. The open entrance foyer spaces extend this threshold internally—spaces for meeting, gathering and orientation leading into the atriums of the hub and business school. The internal environment on a single large-scale building form of expansive meeting and circulation floors is a reference to the Exchange buildings in Manchester— historically trading goods, now the currency is knowledge and learning.

The lower floors around the atrium hallways are for interaction and social learning. The cafes and break-out spaces act as commodious hallways to the lecture theatres positioned strategically at the end of these spaces. The pulse of large groups of students and staff milling around in an internal market place at the foot of three terraces of student services, academic teaching, and workspaces. These upper levels are laced with open stairs connecting open terraces that form more localised breakout interaction spaces. Every opportunity is used to create highly visible and convivial circulation spaces that are usable as didactic learning spaces. This more open framework blurs the boundaries between staff and students, fostering academic cross-fertilisation. A microcosm of urban life, under one roof, that takes its place in the city.

> In each city there is something which links everything, in mutual justification; at the same time there is something which sets everything apart, by mutual influences and obvious exoticisms.
> ALVARO SIZA

CITY IN THE UNIVERSITY.

# PETER CLEGG
# HIGHER EDUCATION:
# REGENERATIVE DESIGN

More than virtually any other sector of architectural design, Higher Education has an exponential power to change society's approach to sustainability. Students have the capacity to challenge our behavioural patterns and the current generation is the first to have had an education in sustainability at school and are keen to put that into practice. Some will be interested in challenging the attitude of their institutions; others may themselves need to be challenged to take environmental ideas seriously. Universities can benefit from, as well as help develop, environmental awareness; they need to be acting as facilitators in the move towards a more sustainable society.

The triple bottom line of economic, social and environmental sustainability needs to be understood in its widest sense, and we will only begin to be truly innovative when we take an approach which is not only solving the currently defined problems but healing the social and environmental systems that we have recently disrupted. When this happens we will begin to move towards a new paradigm of regenerative architecture and urban design.[1] In the three projects we are examining here we can begin to see the first signs of these changes coming into place as new buildings help to create new urban education communities out of damaged inner areas of our cities.

## ECONOMIC REGENERATION

As economic value transfers from manufacturing to the creative and research-based industries, universities become more significant as economic drivers. In many of our major cities universities are the major employers, providing 1.2 per cent of all employment in the UK, somewhere between accountancy and legal services.[2] And for every ten academic positions there are 12 non-academic jobs in our universities as a whole. Higher Education is a major industry that is key to the future of our urban economy.

It is also changing at a phenomenal rate. Over the ten years from 1999 to 2009, student numbers increased by 44 per cent and, though the impact of tuition fees is yet to be fully assessed, it is likely that the current increase in the proportion of foreign students will continue to grow and we will remain with a student population of around 2,500,000.[3] But courses and departments ebb and flow and building uses change with changes in learning methods and pedagogies. So more and more we are required as architects to produce flexible accommodation that can accommodate a multitude of uses and maintain flexibility on a year-on-year basis.

Our three projects illustrate this each in their own way. At Manchester, though the brief was for a student hub and a business school, the plan arrangements are very similar, with 12 metre deep floor plates adjacent to 12 metre wide light atria providing daylight and ventilation. The building form is eminently flexible with servicing to each floor and column-free flat slabs throughout. At Leeds this requirement was taken one stage further because the building had to be institutionally funded and the entire academic space is based on a 15 metre deep floor plate winding its way around the perimeter of the site and enclosing a central plaza. The building is designed to the institutionally funded norms specified by the British Council of Offices (in relation to partitioning, servicing, floor loading, etc.) so that, should the university decide to discontinue its leasehold arrangement, the funder could look to the commercial market to secure an alternative tenant. Worcester is perhaps the most prescriptive of the three buildings, given its use as a library and archive but even here the deep floor plates with natural light and ventilation ensure that the building could be adapted to future changes in use and certainly to changes in the requirements for a city library.

Flexibility is indeed a major issue on the sustainability agenda. If our buildings are not adaptable to change then the carbon cost of demolition and rebuilding is highly significant. We used to assume that the embodied energy of a building was equivalent to about ten years of the operational energy costs but, as we tighten up on the running costs by building lower energy buildings, so the embodied energy becomes relatively more significant. A recent study we carried out on the refurbishment vs rebuilding costs of a central London office building showed it would take 80 years before the total cumulative operational energy costs were equivalent to the cost of rebuilding the building. In all of the projects we are discussing the sites were previously occupied by very low quality buildings that were incapable of redevelopment and the added value brought huge economic benefit to the infrastructure of the university and the city, but we must assume we are designing to enable future adaptation to the patterns of use as well as to changes in society, technology and indeed climate.

## SOCIAL REGENERATION

Over the last 50 years our cities have gone through a process of shedding dwellings from the centre to the suburbs. Moving from workspaces by day to dormitories by night is wasteful in terms of time and transport energy and leads to underutilisation of space and dead areas of the city at different times of day and night. The influx of an urban student population reverses that trend providing 24 hour life in the city centre. The suburban ivory towers of campus universities segregated academic life from urban life and in the process devalued both. The new metropolitan universities are more integrated and have the advantage of being able to contribute more intimately to social development, feeding off and into the multicultural mix of the cities that house them.

We have always been sceptical of 'university quarters', even more so of student ghettos, but we need to balance the needs of institutions to create efficient environments with the preference for total integration. Labelling creates segregation not the synergy of integration.

At Broadcasting Place for Leeds Metropolitan University (LMU) we wanted to create a living and working 24 hour piece of university. The scheme brings together not only three departments of one faculty but also rehouses a Baptist church that occupied a low grade building on the site. Crucially it also includes 300 student rooms in a tower that marks the corner of the site where it meets the inner ring road of the city. The new development also creates a pedestrian plaza at the centre of the site, integrates the adjacent eighteenth century Friends Meeting House which is also converted for university use, and provides a new public route from the educational facilities to the north of the site through to the city centre.

Part of the brief for the building at Manchester Metropolitan University (MMU) was to provide a student hub for a university that is fully integrated into its urban context. The university's site here is quite constrained and the new building forms a corner piece to the campus defined by Grosvenor Square and in the process forms a signboard to the busy Mancunian Way. MMU has a policy of using sites throughout the city, certainly in its integration with the creative industries, but decentralisation requires a

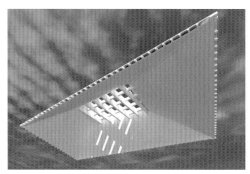

strong student hub to provide a one-stop-shop for all the student services. As patterns of learning change so the extent and significance of social learning spaces increases. The city's cafes and social spaces can be colonised by the universities as an extension of the campus just as housing and shops feed off and supply the student population.

The library at Worcester is an extreme example of integration. The joint brief provides a learning resources facility that is shared by the city and its university in a building dedicated to lifelong learning. It required an integrated vision, a site that ultimately will provide a new pedestrian route through from university to city, with additional developments (currently stalled by the recession) that will increase connectivity and extend the pedestrian realm within the city. In all these examples we are healing and developing the city rather than creating segregated facilities typical of the campus plans of 50 years ago.

## ENVIRONMENTAL REGENERATION

As architects we have a duty of care not only to minimise the impact of our buildings on global warming but to move society towards a greater commitment to carbon reduction. We need to provide buildings which use less energy but educate people to use less energy in them. It is not just a question of the efficiency of the building but of the capacity of the building to stimulate further change: the system boundaries we are dealing with need to go beyond the construction project.

Given the HEFCE commitment to reduce carbon emissions from universities by 34 per cent by 2020 and 80 per cent by 2050 this seems at first to be an unrealistic target.[4] But the UK government's Zero Carbon Task Force for schools looked at the problem from a different perspective and Bill Bordass, who was part of that task force, came up with the following methodology: "halve the energy demand, double the efficiency of the equipment and take half the carbon out of the supply and you are down to one eighth of the carbon emissions."[5] Suddenly, broken down into bite sized chunks, the task becomes more realisable.

The starting point has to be the way our buildings use energy on a daily basis. The chart opposite shows the anticipated carbon emissions for each of our three buildings, in comparison with various benchmarks. The figures represent substantial improvements over the 'notional' buildings which form the test but they represent the regulated loads only and do not take into account issues such as extended hours of operation, management and maintenance failings, as well as the huge burden of 'unregulated' loads in the form of excessive plug loads. We can see that both MMU and the Worcester building have already achieved substantial improvements in performance though these need to be tested via post occupancy evaluation. Based on the 'actual' building loads of MMU for instance the energy costs would be approximately 30 kWh/m$^2$ and we know from data from the sector review of Higher Education policy that the average value of energy use across the sector is almost ten times that value at 287 kWh/m$^2$.[6] What is significant for all these buildings is that the heating loads have reduced dramatically and we are left with a building energy use that is dominated by lighting and auxiliary energy and small power loads. So having all but eliminated the heating load, electricity has become by far the major source of energy used in the building.

But the building form and skin are the primary consideration for any low energy building. Given that daylight and ventilation are more significant than heating as drivers of energy performance the challenge is how to get light and air into the depths of the plan.

**top and bottom** Worcester 'Hive': Roof geometry and shading grid. The irregular geometry of the truncated pyramid roofs are united by the shading grid which forms the structural ring beam to the top of each rooflight. Parametric modelling predicted that bursts of sunlight might hit the roof itself but not cause glare into the spaces below.

**opposite** Comparative annual carbon dioxide emissions for each of the three buildings in comparison with various Higher Education Environmental Performance Indicators (www. heepi.org). All figures are based on the Part L 2A (2006) Criterion 1 and Energy Performance Certificate (EPC) Assessment procedures.

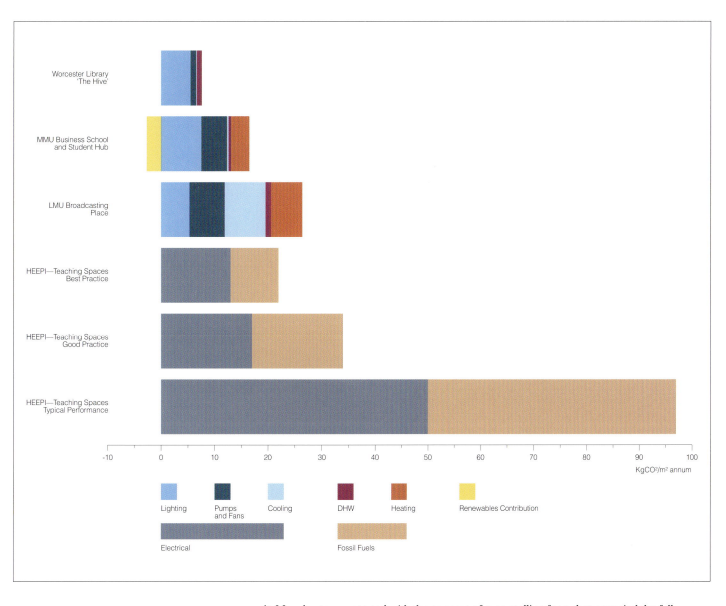

| | | | | | |
|---|---|---|---|---|---|
| Lighting | Pumps and Fans | Cooling | DHW | Heating | Renewables Contribution |

Electrical

Fossil Fuels

KgCO²/m² annum

At Manchester we started with the concept of a crystalline form that occupied the full extent of the corner site and provided us with an active roof, or capturing sunlight and daylight with walls clad in a self shading 'pleated' crystalline skin. Slicing the building with two east–west facing atria allows daylight to penetrate to the ground floor and provides a return airpath for the ventilation system. A square metre of rooflight is about three times as efficient as a window at admitting daylight and it is easier to control solar gain via internal shading [see p. 28].

At Worcester the dominant roof forms are also devices to capture daylight and enhance, in this case, wind-assisted natural ventilation. The irregular geometry of the truncated pyramidal forms all share the same regular geometrical shading grid that forms the structure of the rooflight, carefully calculated to cut out glare from all sensitive areas but allow a burst of occasional sunlight into those areas where it would be appreciated. Parametric modelling was key to defining the sunlight penetration as well as helping with the calculation of the structural spanning characteristics of the roof panels.

South-western

| SW - Jun 21 | SW - Sept 21 | SW - Dec 21 | SW - Mar 21 |

Western

| W - Jun 21 | W - Sept 21 | W - Dec 21 | W - Mar 21 |

North-western

| NW - Jun 21 | NW - Sept 21 | NW - Dec 21 | NW - Mar 21 |

South-eastern

| SE - Jun 21 | SE - Sept 21 | SE - Dec 21 | SE - Mar 21 |

Eastern

| E - Jun 21 | E - Sept 21 | E - Dec 21 | E - Mar 21 |

North-eastern

| NE - Jun 21 | NE - Sept 21 | NE - Dec 21 | NE - Mar 21 |

Manchester Metropolitan University Business School and Student Hub daylighting concept. Incident solar radiation studies on the six facades of the building. Shading provided by a 'pleated' facade was calculated to reduce solar gain and cooling loads by 15 per cent.

**opposite** LMU elevational studies. Studies of two out of the 17 elevations of the Broadcasting Place project showing the development from preliminary calculations of incident solar radiation through a series of algorithms to produce a facade with appropriate percentages and patterns of glazing.

LEEDS METROPOLITAN UNIVERSITY: Daylighting and Solar Gain Analysis and Facade Modelling

1a. Glazing percentage required to achieve 3% average daylight factor

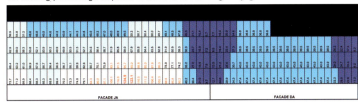

| 00% | DF less than 2% |
|---|---|
| 00% | DF less than 2% and 3% |
| 00% | All panels glazed |
| 00% | 3 out of 4 panels glazed |
| 00% | 2 out of 4 panels glazed |
| 00% | 1 out of 4 panels glazed |

1a. Maximum percentage glazing possible without overheating

| 00% | All panels glazed |
|---|---|
| 00% | 3 out of 4 panels glazed |
| 00% | 2 out of 4 panels glazed |
| 00% | 1 out of 4 panels glazed |

2. Comparative analysis and daylighting is overheating: the need for solar glass

| 00% | Standard glazing is OK |
|---|---|
| 00% | Pilkington Suncool or equivalent glass required |
| 00% | 3% Daylight overheats (with solar glass), 2% is OK |
| 00% | 2% Daylight overheats |

3. Final glazing ratios

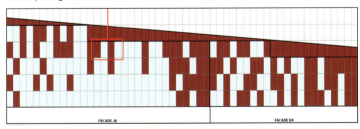

| 00% | DF < 2%, or overheating |
|---|---|
| 00% | DF between 2% and 3% |
| 00% | All panels glazed, DF = 3% |
| 00% | 3 out of 4 panels glazed, DF = 3% |
| 00% | 2 out of 4 panels glazed, DF = 3% |
| 00% | 1 out of 4 panels glazed, DF = 3% |

4. Computer generated facade based on the 3x1.5m module

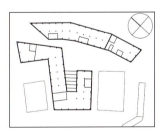

4. Final facade: with a higher grain of modules added

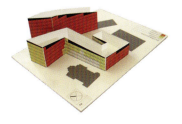

At Leeds, the problem was one of defining the percentage of glazing that was appropriate to the 17 different facade orientations, each of which was also shaded by surrounding buildings. So working with the BRE we developed a programme to evaluate the appropriate percentage of glazing on a series of defined 'cells' covering the facade of the building to generate a four per cent daylight factor as well as avoid the risks of solar gain. Inevitably this provides a facade that allows for more glazing at lower levels where there is shading from surrounding buildings and a lower percentage at higher levels where the sky component of the daylight factor is greater, and begins to suggest a motif for the cladding of the building [see p. 29].

In urban situations it is more and more of a challenge to get access to fresh air unpolluted by fumes and noise. At MMU the bulk of the facade faces an urban motorway so the idea of a naturally ventilated building was dismissed very early on in the design process; the challenge then became how to make the mechanical ventilation system work most efficiently. Large ducts, straight runs, displacement ventilation, atrium return airpaths and rooftop plant with heat recovery all followed as a consequence.

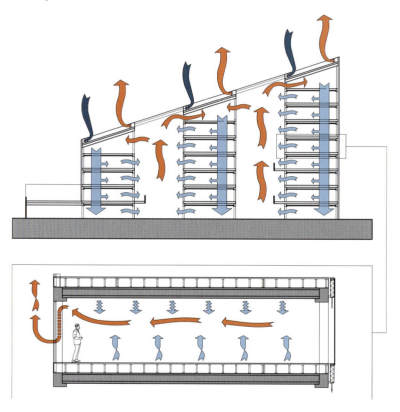

MMU Business School and Student Hub: Air distribution. Air is distributed via displacement ventilation through raised floor zones and thence via attenuated ducts within the acoustically insulated wall panels through to both atria which, in turn, provide a return air space to the roof top plant rooms. Radiant cooling is built into ceiling panels at each level.

At Worcester we had much less traffic noise and pollution, and natural ventilation becomes a driver of the design with air intake via BMS controlled windows at the perimeter (with shading on the south elevation that also provides acoustic attenuation to the openable windows) and via a four square metre underground duct that emerges in the centre of the building. Extract is controlled at high level with louvres on each side of the truncated pyramids that are protected by an outer layer of cladding from being subject to unequal wind pressure. Air tunnel tests confirmed that the effect of wind would be to enhance the extract rate rather than cause downdrafts in the roof spaces.

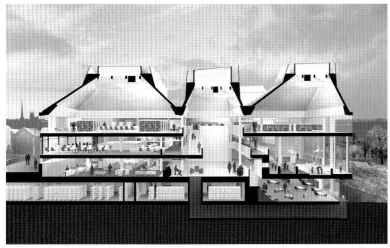

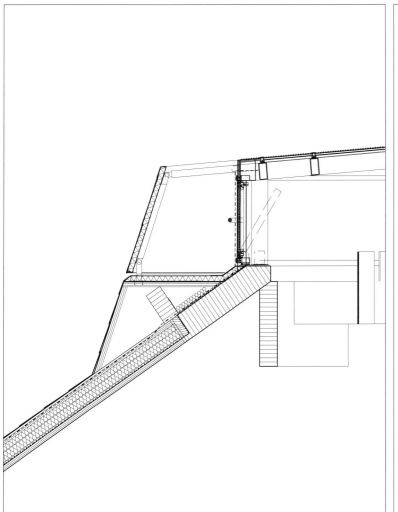
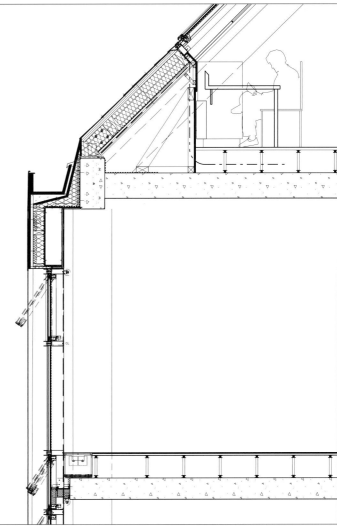

<u>clockwise from top left</u> Worcester 'Hive': Overall Cross-section of the building from south to north; wind tunnel testing of roof forms; south elevation light shelves and acoustical attenuation panels adjacent to open windows; walkway at high level providing access to inward opening roof vents at the top of each pyramid.

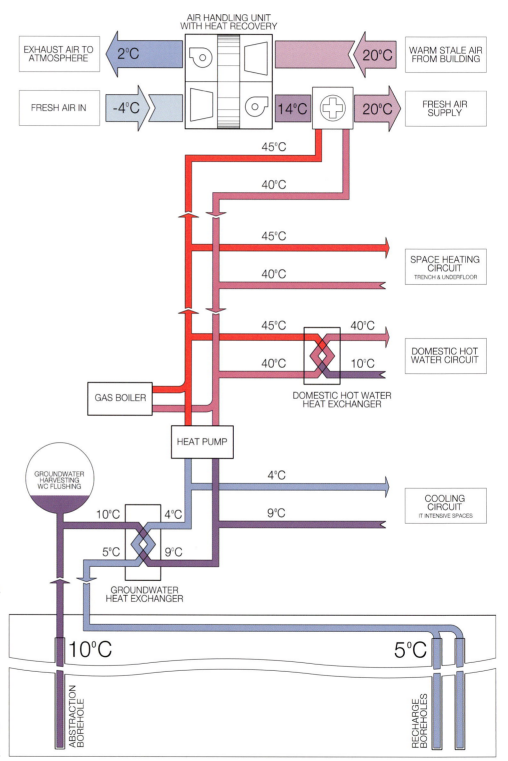

MMU Business School and Student Hub: Ground source heat pump; winter mode (right); MMU: Ground source heat pump; summer mode (opposite). Source: AECOM.

In summer water is abstracted from the bore hole at 12°C and provides direct cooling to the beams in the ceilings. Return water form the ceiling provides a supply to the heat pump to drive the domestic hot water circuit, and cooling to the fresh air supply when required. In winter, the ground water is used to provide cooling in intensively-used spaces, but primarily provides a source of energy for the heat pump which is used for space heating and domestic hot water.

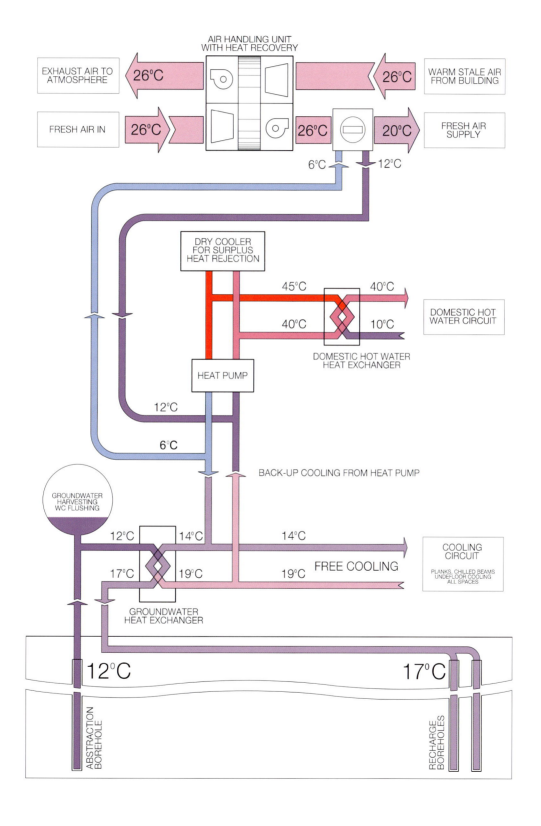

AIR HANDLING UNIT
WITH HEAT RECOVERY

EXHAUST AIR TO
ATMOSPHERE      26°C          26°C      WARM STALE AIR
                                        FROM BUILDING

FRESH AIR IN      26°C        26°C      20°C      FRESH AIR
                                                  SUPPLY

6°C      12°C

DRY COOLER
FOR SURPLUS
HEAT REJECTION

45°C      40°C      DOMESTIC HOT
                    WATER CIRCUIT
40°C      10°C

DOMESTIC HOT WATER
HEAT EXCHANGER

HEAT PUMP

12°C

6°C

BACK-UP COOLING FROM HEAT PUMP

GROUNDWATER
HARVESTING
WC FLUSHING

12°C      14°C          14°C              COOLING
                                          CIRCUIT
17°C      19°C          19°C    FREE COOLING    PLANKS, CHILLED BEAMS
                                                UNDERFLOOR COOLING
                                                ALL SPACES

GROUNDWATER
HEAT EXCHANGER

12°C                                    17°C

ABSTRACTION
BOREHOLE

RECHARGE
BOREHOLES

Although heating energy costs are relatively small compared to electrical loads, cooling loads can become excessive with high computer and appliance loads. So we need to make use of the free ambient cooling that is available. At both LMU and MMU we use ground water (at a constant temperature of around 12°C) to provide an energy source for a heat pump. Heat pumps are extremely useful in that they can provide both heating and cooling energy but are dependent on electrical energy to boost the low grade ground source energy. At Manchester we avoid this by using free cooling direct from the ground in the ceilings of the floorslabs to reduce internal temperatures. The same water source feeds a heat pump to supply cooling to the areas of the building such as server rooms and lecture theatres which have an excessive heat load [see pp. 32–33]. At Worcester we use water from the river, at a similar temperature again to cool the slabs directly but also to supply chilled beams via a heat pump. The underground air intake also contributes to precooling in summer.

All of the above measures are to do with demand reduction, but we also need to look at increasing efficiency. The toughest area to control here is the electrical use and the biggest culprits are computers and IT equipment. MMU recognised this and signed up to a policy which in effect meant that traditional PCs were banished and only 'thin client' networked machines or laptops would be allowed in the building, thus reducing the loads by 70 to 90 per cent. At long last the university community is waking up to the impact of these unregulated loads. The work of the Higher Education Environmental Performance Improvement (www.heepi.org.uk) initiative provides extremely useful baseline data and advice.

Finally there is the question of reducing the carbon in the supply. With the heating system at Worcester this is done by a biomass boiler at the north-west corner of the site, with the capacity to service not only the library but also the proposed future retail and commercial developments. At MMU the south-facing roof slopes which are not glazed for daylighting the atria are covered with 920 square metres of photovoltaic cells. This, combined with the contribution made to heating and cooling via a ground source heat pump, ensured we were able to deliver 18.5 per cent carbon reductions from on-site renewable energy sources.

Low energy design and renewable energy systems cost money; but the key to reducing costs is in the integration of the systems. So for instance at MMU we developed an integrated solution to the construction of the floor slabs that gave us an economical way of spanning 12 metres (and enhanced the flexibility of subdivision of the floor plates), saved carbon intensive concrete by substituting the cement with blast furnace slag and used bubbledeck void formers to reduce weight and embodied energy. Importantly they also incorporated prefabricated cooling pipework in the 'biscuit' layer that formed the high quality permanent shuttering for the floor slabs. Each design decision saves embodied energy and operational energy and results in the floorslab being a critical element of design.

At Worcester the same synergy emerges from the design of the pyramidal roof forms. The change from the initial engineering system based on steel to a solid cross-laminated timber construction was calculated to save between two and 20 years of operational energy of the building (depending on whether you allow or not for the sequestered $CO_2$ in the timber structure). But the roof forms themselves are also essential in terms of their contribution to natural daylight and ventilation as well as their internal visual impact and their iconic form which gives the public building its unique sense of identity.

So just as we depend on integration of patterns of use and building typologies to produce healthy cities, integration of architecture and engineering produces healthy and efficient buildings—buildings which will survive the test of time and the need for constant adaptation and regeneration to a changing society, changing technology and inevitably perhaps a changing climate.

1. Cole, Raymond J (ed.), "Regenerative Design and Development" in *Building Research and Information*, vol. 40, no. 1, London: Routledge, February 2012.
2. Kelly, Ursula, Donald Mclellan and Iain McNicoll, "The impact of universities on the UK economy", Universities UK, 2009.
3. Decade ends with record student numbers. Information from the Universities and Colleges Admissions System (UCAS), 21 January 2010, www.ucas.ac.uk.
4. Carbon Reduction Target and Strategy for Higher Education in England, January 2012, published by the Higher Education Funding Council for England (HEFCE), www.hefce.ac.uk.
5. "The road to zero carbon: final report of the Zero Carbon Force", Department for Education, ref: DCSF00111.2010, January 2010.
6. "Performance in Higher Education Estates: EMS Annual Report 2010", Higher Education Funding Council for England, 2011.

# FEILDEN CLEGG BRADLEY STUDIOS EDUCATION ARCHITECTURE URBANISM THREE UNIVERSITY PROJECTS

SIMON DOODY
MANCHESTER METROPOLITAN
UNIVERSITY BUSINESS SCHOOL
AND STUDENT HUB

38

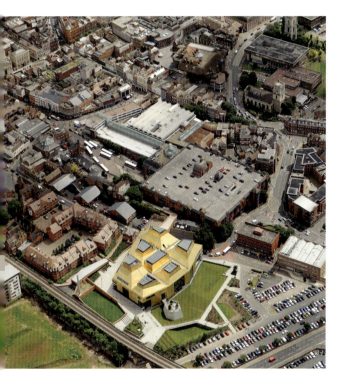

37

JO WRIGHT
THE HIVE
UNIVERSITY OF WORCESTER

ALEX WHITBREAD
BROADCASTING PLACE
LEEDS METROPOLITAN
UNIVERSITY

62

88

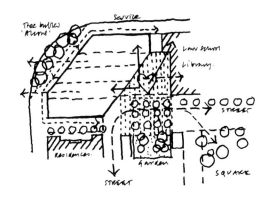

External routes & spaces

# MANCHESTER METROPOLITAN UNIVERSITY BUSINESS SCHOOL AND STUDENT HUB

Manchester Metropolitan University's new Business School and Student Hub is the most significant real estate investment for the university since the 1960s. Commissioned by a new metropolitan university, it has been borne out of an extrovert community-oriented and business-integrated institution that sees itself as the antithesis of its 'cloistered' academic contemporaries. Coupled with it being borne into the new era of fee-paying students with institutions vying to attract students with better course offerings and better facilities, it is an ambitious project that responds to the cultural swings and economic demands that the Higher Education sector faces today.

The brief for the building consisted of two components: a new faculty and a student hub. The larger part, the business school faculty brief was, in the main, fairly standard. It included a number of set piece teaching spaces, including seminar rooms, lecture theatres and IT labs. Complementing those spaces were administrative offices, academic offices and PhD spaces. Binding all these areas together was a requirement for non-standard, 'social learning space'. The Hub brief was to provide the facilities to form the student, academic and pastoral heart to the All Saints Campus—which in turn is the central site in MMU's estate consolidation from six disparate campuses down to three. Spaces to be provided included a one-stop-shop, cafe and catering facilities; large, centrally bookable lecture theatres; counselling facilities, and a whole series of informal social and study spaces. In a city populated by historic trading 'Exchanges', it is these informal spaces we considered as forming the modern Manchester Exchange —the focus for the exchange of ideas and information.

## A MULTI-FACETED APPROACH

In developing the form, aesthetic and character of the scheme, the language of the architecture evolved out of a number of questions. How could a building physically manifest an expression of the ambitious university and how could it reflect its 'extrovert' attitude? Secondly, how could we create a study environment akin to the work environments students will graduate into? Beyond the university, there were questions of how to build in a city with high ambitions for its future development and whether it could catalyse the regeneration of the All Saints Campus. Finally we considered the question of how to create a building to attract a new generation of students from both home and abroad.

The early move of generating a single volume diamond form answered the questions of presence and iconicity. It also created a volume in which its diverse spaces could be hosted in a carved interior that included two large atria—enclosed public space appropriate for Manchester's climate. The big volume building is no stranger to Manchester which hosts a number of grand projects from as early as the Victorian era. Simple in volume, it also has a complexity and unique character derived from the articulation of the facades and the use of as-finished materials that define the interiors to the building.

## FORM—THE RESPONSIVE OBJECT

The building has been described as a 'lodged jewel' holding the corner of the site, offering the varying scales of its facets to the different contexts they address. The

opposite Detail of the building's 'pleated glass' facade with its light refracting dichroic fins.

top Concept for the unlocking of the site with the insertion of the trapezoid building.

bottom Manchester Central Station, constructed in 1880. One of the city's monumental buildings that are integral to its character and skyline.

wedge shape of this section of the building is a direct response to the contextual change in scale from the taller 'city' side of the site to the lower 'university' side. To the northern edge, the building steps up to seven storeys and a simple grand facade has the presence and form to be appreciated by passing traffic. Stepping down to four storeys at its southern edge, it drops to the scale of the adjacent red brick university buildings.

The diamond shape of the plan is also a contextual response. To the west side it cuts away in response to the Cambridge Street interchange. With an equal gesture to the east side it opens up a 45-degree corner to All Saints Square, not only presenting a facade that addresses the square from its recessed position, but opens up a new square behind the existing Bellhouse building and encourages the flow of pedestrians onto the site from Ormond Street.

## THE RESPONSIVE FLOOR PLATE
The building is very simply planned as three parallel, 12 metre wide, 'flexible' floor plates. Spaced apart equally, the floor plates in turn create two 12 metre wide atria. The resulting taller atrium is occupied by the business school and the smaller, by the student hub.

**top** Early sketch for the entrance approach incorporating a covered colonnade.

**bottom** The disposition of the Hub and Business School within the single volume building, each one organised around their own atrium.

**opposite** The atria incorporate a variety of informal spaces that facilitate interaction between the many different building users.

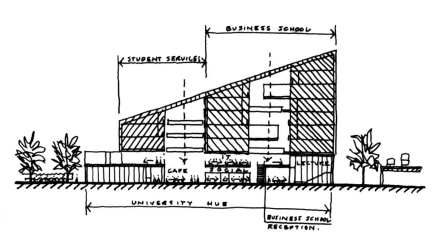

At the ground and first floor, the key student interfacing functions are clustered around and in the atria—including a large group learning space, a one-stop-shop enquiry desk, accommodation and IT offices, IT drop-in spaces, a food outlet and a coffee shop that also spills out onto the new square. The ground and first floors also house the large lecture theatres, with the three largest (250 person lecture theatres) located at the ends of each wing at ground floor level to ensure that the large volumes of students can be handled in designated spill-out spaces in the atria bases.

The ground and first floor levels form the base, articulated behind the black concrete facades. This double-height facade treatment captures the 'energy and service wing' to the south of the building, and wraps into a podium linking element that provides a covered colonnaded entrance, a new double-height resource space, and a new entrance to the Law School with the future option to open into the adjacent library.

The mid levels of the building house the bulk of the seminar room spaces as well as the office spaces for the student and academic services teams. The upper levels then accommodate three floors of academic offices in the north wing, with the uppermost floor housing a specialist post-graduate teaching and learning suite, supported by separate break-out and social spaces.

The development of a 12 metre clear spanning floor structure allows the floors to be planned out in a number of different ways, from a 250 person lecture theatre, down to a 60 person seminar room and right down to a single person office. This not only has provided the university with a very responsive, flexible building, but has also allowed the design to change through the process (with whole floors being interchanged), without the requirement for a wholesale re-design of the building.

## THE 'SPACES BETWEEN'

Permeating all levels of the building is a series of informal and formal 'social learning spaces' that provide environments for individual learning, group learning, touchdown, informal teaching and also for socialising. These spaces are the 'glue' that allow interaction between subjects and between students and staff. They are found at the atrium bases, on bridges and platforms that cross the atrium, in and around office floor plates and within the podium link space. Balustrades are designed as shelves—offering informal meeting spaces outside the seminar rooms.

Extensive academic and student consultation on the use of these spaces led to the development of a set of defined 'social learning zones'. Each zone is defined by its layout, furniture and fittings, colour schemes, signage and branding—all designed to engender different behavioural patterns and associated noise levels.

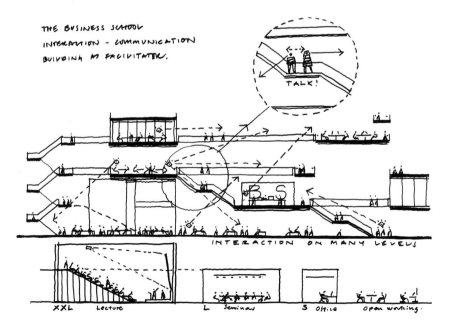

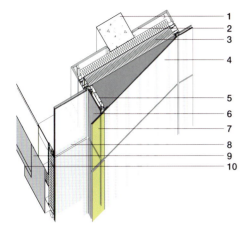

## THE RESPONSIVE FACADE

Wrapping the complete building is the veiling skin. In developing the facade design we collaborated with the artist Martin Richman, to create a unique and distinctive approach.

Contrasting with the red brick buildings of the university precinct, the building was conceived as a glass, crystalline object. 'Pleating' the facade, or veil as it was termed, with light refracting and reflecting dichroic fins, the building takes on an abstract, almost kaleidoscopic appearance. The appearance changes in different ways according to the season and time of day, animating the building even on a grey day, both inside and outside. The volume of the building also changes by day and night. The intention was for the building to take on a homogenous, monumental appearance during the day as the facades reflect. At night, the appearance of the building breaks down as lights turn on inside and activity reveals itself.

The pleats not only articulate the large volume, they serve a functional purpose to shade the facades from low angle sun—especially the large north facade. Putting the cores on the east and west facades further protects the building from low morning and evening sun.

In tune with Manchester's rich heritage of decorative buildings, the new building has its own form of functional decoration. Fritting, to control solar gains, is treated decoratively, with a bar code aesthetic that fades in and out of the 'pleats'.

To deliver the innovative light-refracting element, we worked with Sir Robert McAlpine and Permasteelisa to research a number of different options for encapsulating a material into the projecting fin to the facade. The use of a 3M dichroic film was developed, laboratory tested, site tested and subsequently successfully incorporated into a unitised curtain walling system.

## THE RESPONSIVE TECTONIC

Along with the veil and the heavy black concrete base the building is defined by its third element—a robust exposed concrete skeleton.

In the clear structural expression of the in-situ and pre-cast concrete frame, the resultant interiors reference the tectonics of the local warehouses in Manchester. The reductionist attitude to materials and finishes ensures the interiors have a self-made character, derived from the simple material palette. Again, this was to marry the themes of the corporate workplace with that of the creative independent.

The main structural frame is built from in-situ concrete columns and edge beams, between which an 'Omnicore' flooring system spans. The six main cores are of in-situ concrete, constructed using a self-lifting vertical climbing formwork. For both these structural elements a bespoke concrete mix was developed that incorporated GGBFS (ground and granulated blast furnace slag), replacing 35 per cent of the cement content. This figure was a balance of reducing its embodied energy, allowing quick enough striking times and giving the concrete the warm, light creamy colour we were seeking.

Along with the pre-cast flooring system, the building incorporates a number of other pre-cast elements—the free-standing atrium lift shafts, the atrium glazing 'tracery', atrium roof planks and core stairs. These were all colour matched to the main frame.

opposite top Concept for the two atria and their linking spaces.

opposite bottom Balancing the buildings set piece teaching spaces are a range of informal meeting spaces.

top Detail illustrating the bespoke unitised curtain wall with its projecting glass rainscreen.

1.  In-situ concrete column
2.  Internal plasterboard linings
3.  Unitised Rockwool Lamella insulated curtain wall panel, complete with:
4.  Toughened and laminated glass rainscreen panel with bespoke frit pattern
5.  Anodised aluminium arm—to which glass is structural silicon bonded
6.  Toughened and laminated black back-fritted, reflective glass reveal panel
7.  Dichroic fin—3M radiant film laminated into the glass rainscreen panel
8.  Double glazed, unitised curtain wall vision panel
9.  In-situ concrete edge beam
10. Bespoke, pre-cast Omnia floor system with cast-in cooling pipework

## SUSTAINABILITY — THE INTEGRATED SYSTEM

The building design has focused heavily on carbon reduction, both in terms of its operational energy and its embodied energy. The client's original specification for the project included achieving BREEAM 'excellent', utilising on-site renewable energy sources to offset ten per cent of the building's energy use and an energy use target of 150 kWh/m²/yr.

The completed building has achieved the BREEAM targets, exceeded the target for renewables with a figure closer to 18.5 per cent, and improved upon the energy use target with a figure of 120 kWh/m²/yr. It has also achieved an energy performance certification 'B', which is excellent for this type of high occupancy building with extended hours of use.

Due to the noise of the Mancunian Way, it was determined a sealed building solution was required. With this decision made, the assessment of balancing internal energy loads was undertaken. The deep plan nature of the building and the extensive provision of IT create cooling loads at all times of the year. There is also the potential for significant space heating demands, for example in the atria spaces, particularly as parts of the building can operate on a 24 hour basis. Due to the size of the building, heating and cooling demands can occur concurrently.

As a sealed building, the strategy was developed to ventilate the building via displacement mechanical ventilation, provided to the majority of areas using the raised access floor as a supply plenum. The air that passes up to the plant rooms at roof level has its heat recovered in winter, and rejected in summer.

To deal with the renewables requirements, a ground source heat pump providing heating and cooling was established as the most energy and cost effective solution.

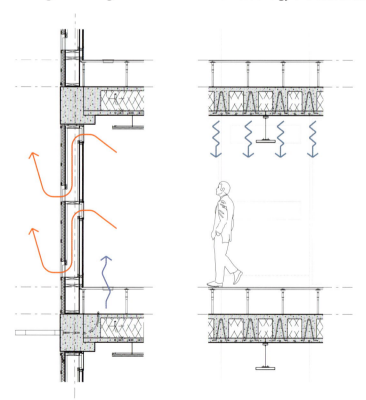

**right** Detail section through a typical section of floor plate, illustrating the innovative, thermally activated building structure — pre-cast, fair-faced Omnia slabs with cast in cooling pipework.

**opposite** Model of the developed scheme submitted in support of the planning application.

The system is open loop, utilising one abstraction borehole and two recharge boreholes. The heating and cooling systems are both served from heat pumps, with the heat pumps operating to move heat from the cooling system to the heating system. This allows heat from areas that require cooling, such as IT rooms, to be used to heat other areas of the building or to be used to pre-heat the domestic hot water supply.

The system is relatively carbon intensive due to the electrical loads of pumps and fans. To off-set this usage is a 920 m$^2$, 128 kWh, photovoltaic installation mounted on the large south-facing roof. Along with daylight and proximity controlled, dimmable lighting, low energy LED lighting and low powered appliances, the client has installed energy efficient IT and printer equipment to reduce small power consumption.

## THE ABSENCE OF VISIBLE SERVICES

In tune with the reductionist attitude to finishes, the coordination and concealment of services was fundamental to a clean visual finish. One of the core innovations of the building was to conceal and coordinate the cooling system into the soffits of the concrete floor slabs—simply by casting cooling pipework into the concrete. Not wanting this to be a site installed operation due to the risk of damage to the team, Sir Robert McAlpine, Hanson and Velta developed a bespoke 1.5 metre wide by 12 metre long 'Omnicore' slab. The pipework was cast into the Omnia element—a 75 mm biscuit slab finished with a percentage of white cement, to give it a high reflectance for day lighting benefits. Great care was taken over the quality of the surface finish to ensure the exposed faces required absolutely no further treatment.

Air is treated in a similar manner. The displacement ventilation system uses the raised floor for supply, with the return air path passing into the atria via acoustic attenuators concealed behind barcode slotted panels that double up as acoustic absorption in the atria. Air rises to the upper atrium levels and is extracted through perforated wall panels into the roof level plant rooms.

The resultant design allows great flexibility with rooms easily added or reconfigured without having to move, or add, mechanical services.

## THE FUTURE OF THE BUILDING

Commissioned to also complete the fit-out, we were given a deeper insight into the university's workings and its culture, and how it was adapting to a rationalisation of its activities that accompanies their estate consolidation. As the new building has been slowly occupied it has already had to be modified in areas to adapt to new uses and shifts in working patterns. The robust, flexible design has easily absorbed these alterations to date. Its future success though, will be measured on its ability to continue to accommodate changes. Inevitably, MMU will proactively evolve to meet any impacts that the evolving Higher Education sector presents.

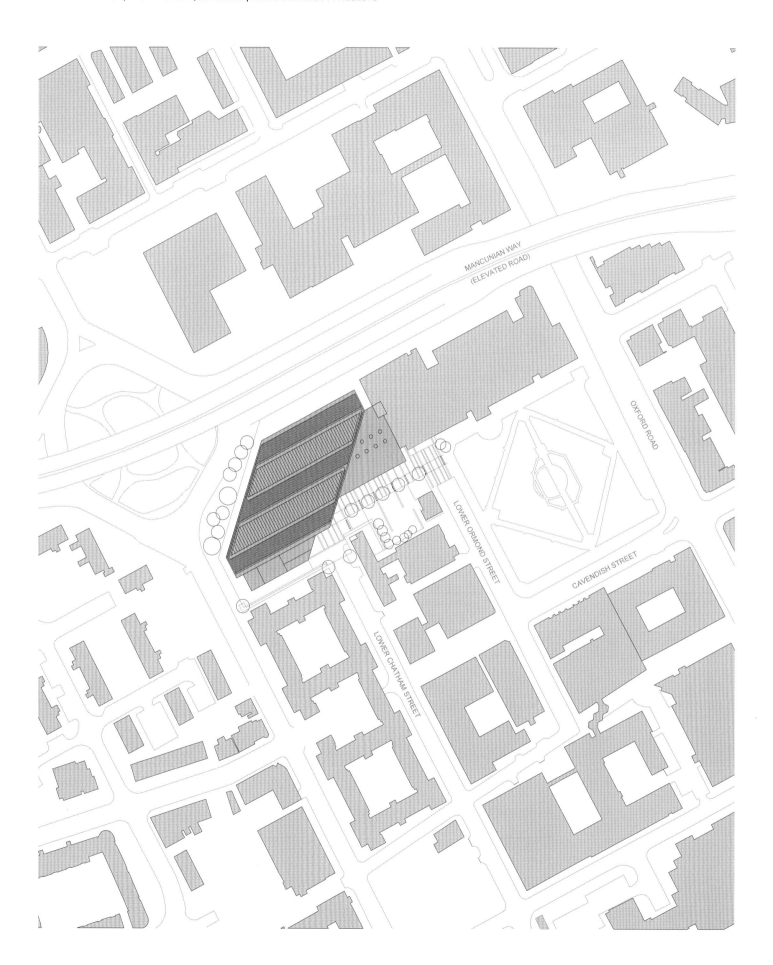

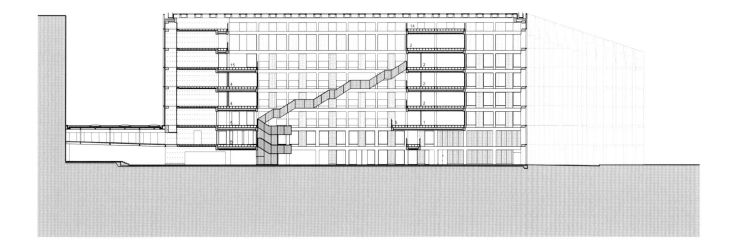

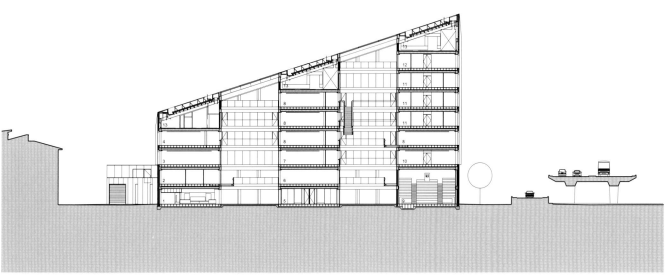

key
1. Cafe
2. Cellular offices
3. SAS offices
4. 30 person seminar room
5. Group room

6. IT office
7. IT lab
8. 60 person seminar room
9. 250 person lecture theatre
10. Business school admin offices

11. Business school academic offices
12. Post-graduate suite
13. Plant room
14. PhD doctoral hot-desk space
15. Social/study space

opposite  Site plan.
top  Cross-section A.
bottom  Cross-section B.

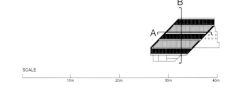

SCALE

10m          20m          30m          40m

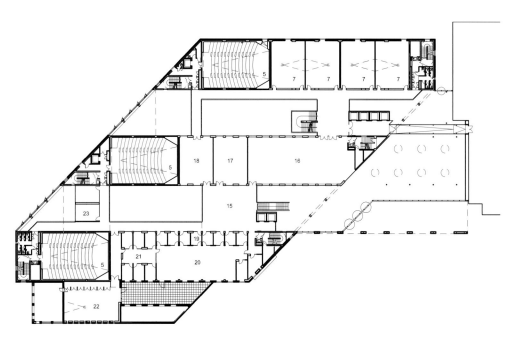

First floor plan

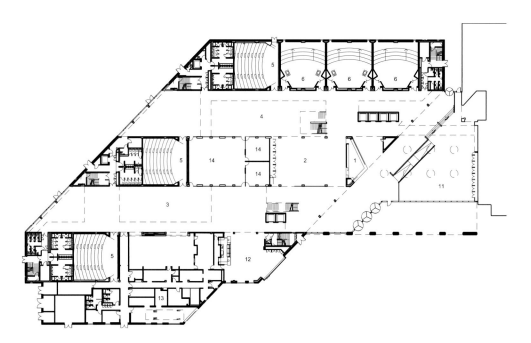

Ground floor plan

| key | 1. | Reception | 8. | 60 person seminar room | 15. | Waiting/meeting space | 22. | Wellbeing room |
|---|---|---|---|---|---|---|---|---|
| | 2. | Consultation zone | 9. | 30 person seminar room | 16. | IT zone | 23. | Meeting room |
| | 3. | Hub atrium/dining | 10. | 45 person seminar room | 17. | Accomodation office | 24. | Executive development room |
| | 4. | Business school atrium/study | 11. | Employability hub | 18. | IT office | 25. | MBA lecture theatre |
| | 5. | 250 person lecture theatre | 12. | Cafe | 19. | Consultation room | 26. | Break-out/study/social spaces |
| | 6. | 120 person lecture theatre | 13. | Kitchen | 20. | SAS offices | 27. | PhD doctoral hot-desk space |
| | 7. | 90 person lecture theatre | 14. | Group study rooms | 21. | Counselling suite | | |

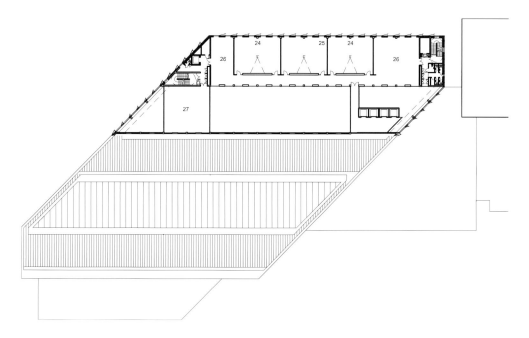

Seventh floor plan

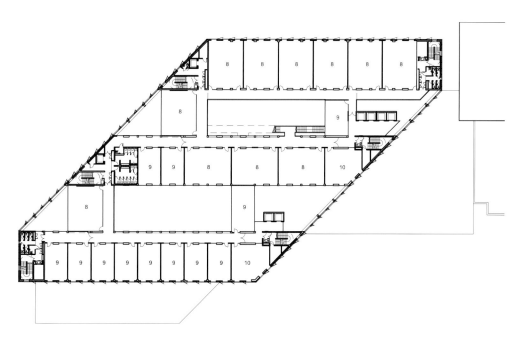

Third floor plan

SCALE

10m      20m      30m      40m      50m

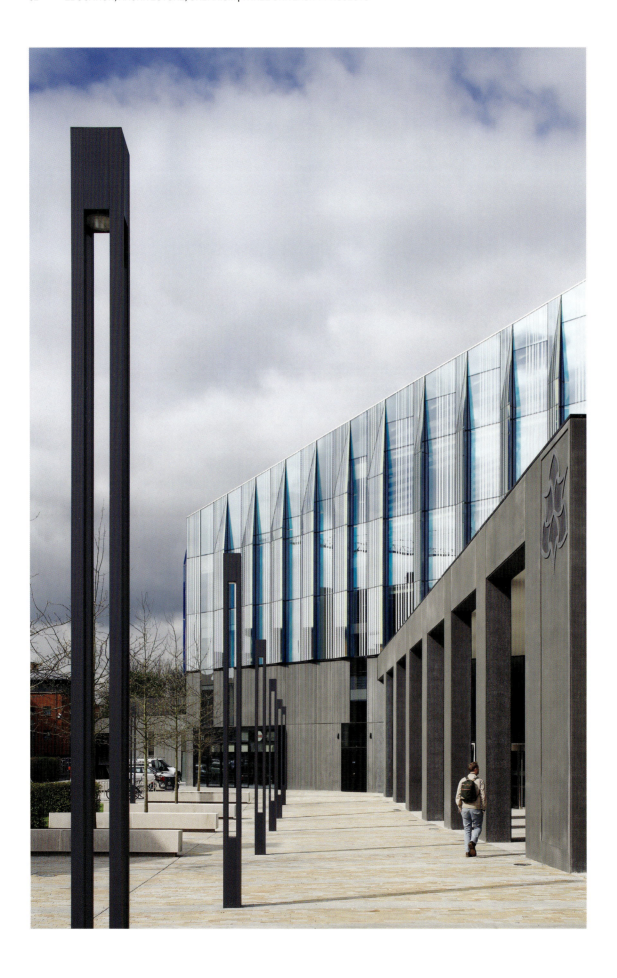

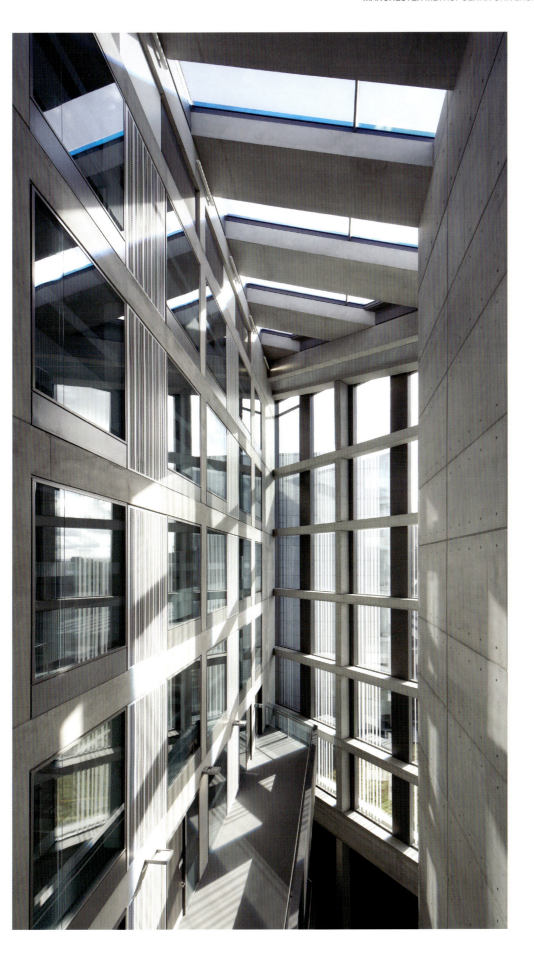

# THE HIVE
# UNIVERSITY OF WORCESTER

The Hive—Worcester Library and History Centre—is the first joint-use library in the UK. It exploits the potential for synergies in the provision of a range of public services 'under one roof', both in terms of operational efficiency and user experience. The project partners created the ambitious vision for this new public amenity with holistic sustainability at its heart.

## PARTNERSHIP WORKING

The Hive has emerged from the unique partnership between the University of Worcester and Worcestershire County Council that was established in 2004. It replaces a range of provisions previously located across the city, uniting them in a single location to create an innovative new typology which exploits the synergies between the services provided to benefit and inspire users and staff.

The procurement through the Private Finance Initiative entailed an extended period of competitive dialogue which fostered positive teamwork and a spirit of partnership between the bid team and the end user representatives. The regular day-long dialogue sessions were as much focused on the evolution of the new organisation as on the emerging design proposals. As the design team crystallised proposals for the building, the end users began to envisage how they might work together in their new home.

## INNOVATION

The Project Partners' vision was to create the first purpose-built, joint-use library in Europe where the city library collection is seamlessly integrated with the university collection to create a single resource for all users. Co-location with the County Archive and Local History Centre has created a unique public facility. The central location lent itself to the inclusion of a Service Centre for the Local Authority which, in addition to meeting the immediate needs of Worcester residents, entices them to explore the wealth of resources on offer at the Hive.

This vision for an agglomeration of public services under one roof is not unique—the rebranding of public libraries as 'Idea Stores' advertised their potential to provide a broader community resource; however the integration with Higher Education is a first in the UK. The architecture reflects the aspiration to be truly accessible—it is deliberately populist in style and highly transparent in the hope that this will encourage the broadest range of visitors to come and explore. It is designed to foster whole-life learning for the entire community, to promote social inclusion by access to education and inspiration and ultimately to be a catalyst for social mobility. This ambition is every bit as innovative as the ambitious environmental sustainability requirements set out in the original brief.

## URBAN DESIGN

The Hive is located just outside the line of the Medieval city wall, immediately to the north of the prominent nineteenth century railway viaduct and some 100 metres to the east of the River Severn, the floodplain of which it abuts. The development presented the opportunity to heal the somewhat eroded fringe of the city with the creation of a new permeable and accessible city block that incorporates significant new public realm and connects the heart of the city to the recently developed University of Worcester Castle Street Campus.

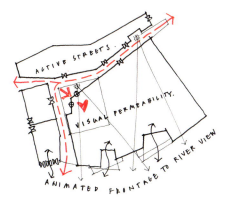

Early site concept plan: The Hive forms part of a new city block with pedestrian streets which are reminiscent of Worcester's historic core, animated by active frontages.

As a significant new public building, the Hive marks the northern boundary of the city centre much as the historic cathedral marks the southern limits; both are prominent from the river valley. As the cathedral is a beacon for faith, the Hive celebrates knowledge, from the repository of the county's rich history to life-long learning for the whole community.

Our design response to the site was to differentiate the Hive from its context whilst using the 5,000 square metres of commercial accommodation anticipated in the brief (though not yet delivered) to provide a foil to the public building: an embracing arm of retail, restaurants and a hotel was intended to ascend from the modest scale of the one building retained on the site up to eaves height of the Hive itself, enclosing a new pedestrian thoroughfare reminiscent in scale and articulation of the alleyways which meander through the historic city. Meanwhile, to the south of The Butts, another small commercial building engaged with the new pedestrian bridge to provide a safe, accessible and animated route connecting the city centre to the university campus.

The landscape setting is inspired by the context, history and ecology of Worcestershire. To the west, in the part of the site that sits within the floodplain, the sculpted landforms are designed to flood periodically, and soft landscape has been selected to tolerate this. Planting motifs within the basins are drawn from historic Royal Worcester pottery designs. The elevated 'island' set within the basins provides secure external space accessed from the children's library. A new landscaped belvedere at the north-western corner of the site provides seating and a location for public gatherings, whilst the new library square marks the main public entrance to the Hive.

## LEARNING ENVIRONMENTS

The brief required a range of study settings ranging from 'active' to 'reflective' in order to provide for the diversity of users anticipated. Early analysis of the site area and the likely footprint suggested that public areas should be arranged over several levels, whilst the desire for physical and intellectual access implied that these should be well connected. This led to the concept of a 'social landscape' with excellent connectivity both horizontally and vertically. A series of atria provide visual connection and allow daylight deep into the plan providing a strong sense of the totality from much of the public zone.

This connectivity, inspired by the aspiration for a truly inclusive building, presented the design team with the challenge of providing an appropriate acoustic environment for each activity and great care has been taken to provide acoustic absorption and, where necessary, separation such that users with very different requirements can happily coexist. The meeting 'pods' that hover over the children's library are acoustically isolated from the noise below whilst sharing the fabulous views out to the river and the Malvern Hills.

The active/reflective gradient runs broadly from west to east rising up through the building. At lower ground floor overlooking the flood basins there is a 'social learning' zone where paper coexists with digital media in a range of settings for group and individual study. Directly above is the children's library where zones are tailored to the needs of different age groups from pre-school to older teens. This shares the entrance level with the quick access library, the Hub, the cafe and a studio theatre to create a dynamic, all-age environment. At first floor the History Centre includes both a secure study area for examination of archive material and an open access collection. At this level there is also a suite of bookable public meeting rooms.

The principal library is at second floor where the six perimeter roof cones imply separate 'reading rooms', each of which provides a subtly different environment with contrasting views and light, accentuated by contrasts in colours used for floors and furniture. Book stack heights are varied to provide differing degrees of enclosure and acoustic environment. Even within this floor plate users can choose a study setting to suit their preferences.

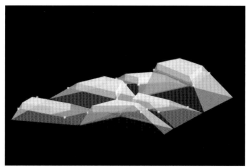 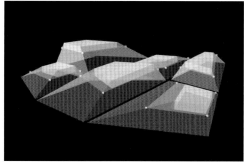 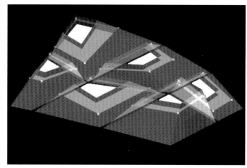

At third floor, a single cone accommodates a silent study area that is completely separate from the rest of the library volume. This 'eyrie' that sits within the cone itself enjoys fabulous views out between the roof forms to the river valley. The laminated timber structure is suddenly within reach, providing yet another contrast in environment.

## SUSTAINABILITY

The Project Partners set pioneering targets for environmental sustainability. They recognised that this prominent new public building has the capacity to educate users by being a sustainable exemplar. The brief required an 'A' rated Energy Performance Certificate and BREEAM 'excellent' as a minimum. It also required a building designed to adapt to the predicted impact of climate change to 2050 (as defined by the UK Climate Impact Programme, UK-CIP) and which reduces $CO_2$ generation by 50 per cent compared to current Building Regulations.

As designers we were encouraged by these aspirations and by the deep understanding of environmental sustainability set out in the brief. Working closely with Max Fordham Partnership we set out to build on our shared experience of delivering highly sustainable and innovative buildings from the New Environmental Office at the BRE and Heelis, the Central Office of the National Trust (a benchmark project identified in the Hive's brief) to the Woodland Trust HQ. Daylight and natural ventilation were central to the success of these earlier buildings. The Hive presented us with the challenge of applying our approach to a larger and more complex building.

Sustainability has informed both form and specification. The Hive is designed to minimise its impact in construction, operation and ultimate disposal. The highly articulated section with multiple atria connecting the principal floor levels introduces daylight deep into the plan via the glazed tops of the seven irregular roof cones. The vertical upstands of the cones incorporate openable vents set within protective baffles. These facilitate natural ventilation whatever the prevailing wind direction, with air intake via the external elevations and a sub-floor duct that delivers tempered air directly to the central atrium. The Hive is cooled in peak conditions using water from the River Severn which passes through soffit-mounted chilled beams, and heated using locally sourced biomass.

Use of Building Information Modelling: We developed bespoke software based on Bentley's Generative Components to explore the design of the roof cones using structural and environmental parameters to ensure that daylighting and natural ventilation criteria were met.

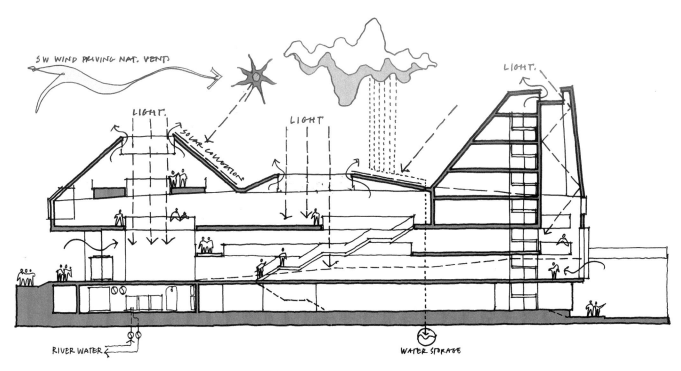

SW WIND DRIVING NAT. VENT

LIGHT.

SOLAR COLLECTOR

LIGHT

LIGHT

LIGHT.

RIVER WATER

WATER STORAGE

**above** Environmental concept section: Sustainability was central to the brief at bid stage—this diagram captures our first thoughts on how the building might exploit daylight and natural ventilation to minimise its environmental impact.

**opposite** 1:500 block model—gold leaf on plaster. Made at bid stage to communicate the impact of the scaly golden carapace, this model which fits in the palm of a hand was passed around the table in the Competitive Dialogue process allowing end users to contemplate the three dimensional form from every angle.

The concrete frame incorporates GGBFS in lieu of 50 per cent of the cement content, thus reducing embodied energy. The roof cones which were initially designed in steel and concrete were reconceived in solid laminated timber generated a $CO_2$ saving in excess of 2,000 tonnes compared to the original approach. This was achieved using award-winning, bespoke software developed by our team which incorporated structural and environmental parameters and allowed us to manipulate the forms of the roof cones to achieve the desired internal environment whilst minimising material use.

Wherever possible materials were sourced locally; Forrest of Dean Pennant forms the plinth and the public realm and locally-sourced bricks are used in the adjacent structures, echoing the materials of the historic city fabric. The carapace of copper alloy shingles, though not locally manufactured, is durable and entirely recyclable.

The Hive has exceeded its brief requirements and is anticipated to be rated as 'outstanding' under BREEAM 2008.

### ACCESSIBILITY
The Hive is designed to be truly accessible to all its users and visitors and to improve the connectivity of the city centre by providing accessible routes linking the disparate existing levels. The ramped pedestrian street that encircles the building provides this parity of access whilst, inside, design decisions were guided by consultation with the Worcestershire Access Group whose members reviewed emerging proposals to ensure that their needs were met.

We explored the concept of 'intellectual access' and set out to create an interior that is easy to navigate despite the complexity of the brief, such that even unfamiliar users are encouraged to explore. Visual and physical connectivity throughout the public areas of the building, legible vertical circulation and orientation provided by the central atrium make for simple navigation of the public areas.

## COMPLEXITY AND SPECIFICITY

The brief for the Hive required the provision of highly specific facilities for each of the end user groups. Our design response accommodates these in a configuration that also responds to the setting, aspect, orientation and access to the site and which balances the drama and delight of the public spaces with the functionality of the 'back of house' areas. Staff range from librarians to Service Centre staff, archaeologists and archivists, and each has subtly different needs from their workspace.

## CONCLUSIONS

The Hive is a unique response to a challenging, inspiring and very specific brief that responds to the opportunities and constraints of the site. Its architecture, both internally and externally, is an expression of these particular stimuli rather than a manifestation of any particular 'style'. It is unashamedly of its time, celebrating the place of learning in the twenty-first century city as the cathedral marks the place of faith in the Medieval city.

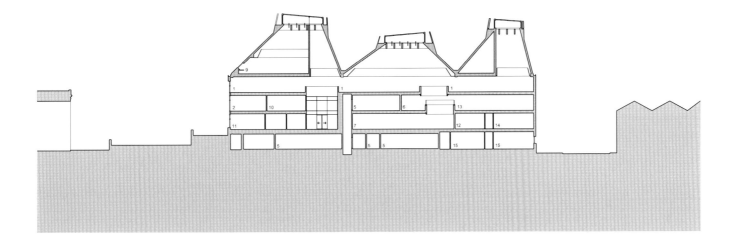

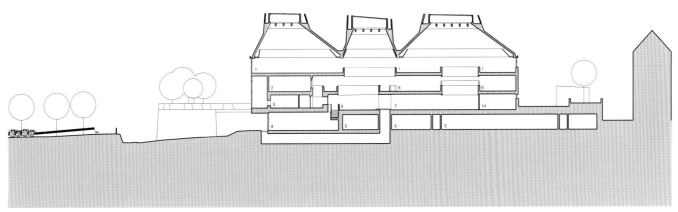

key
1.  Library/Study
2.  Meeting rooms
3.  Childen's library
4.  Youth library
5.  Archive
6.  Original documents consultation
7.  Hub
8.  Quick access
9.  Quiet study
10. Business lounge
11. Cafe
12. Interview rooms
13. History
14. Staff area
15. Archaeology

opposite  Site plan.
top       Cross-section north–south A.
bottom    Cross-section west–east B.

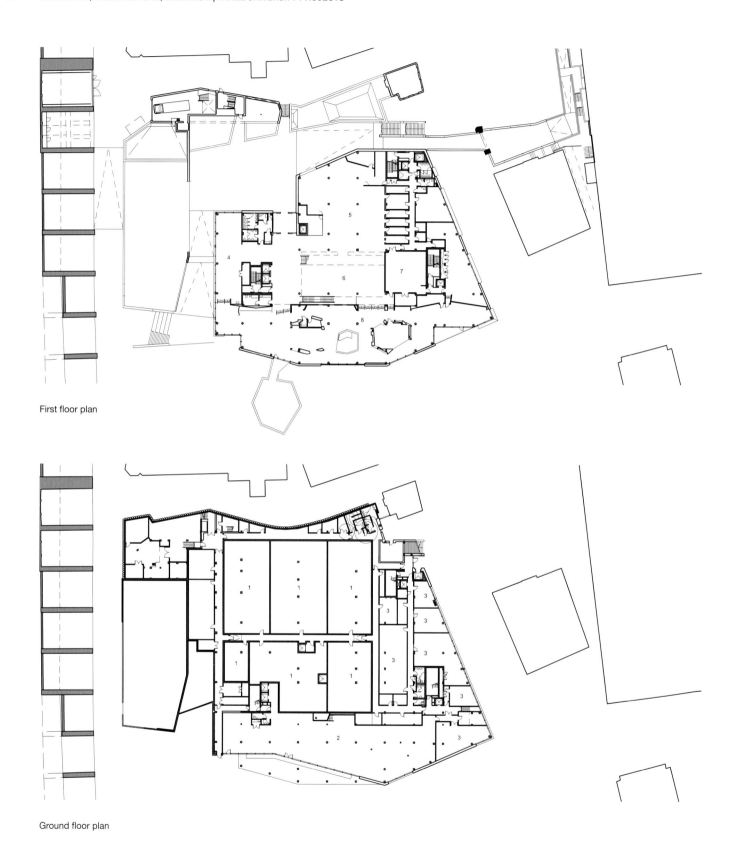

First floor plan

Ground floor plan

key  1. Archive                    5. Hub                    9. Meeting room                       13. Staff area
     2. Youth library              6. Quick access           10. Business lounge                  14. Library/study
     3. Archaeology                7. Studio/lecture theatre  11. Original documents consultation  15. Quiet study
     4. Cafe                       8. Children's library     12. History                          16. Social learning

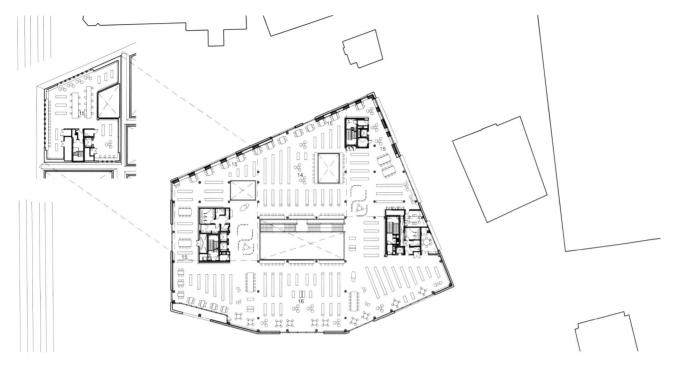

Third/fourth floor plan

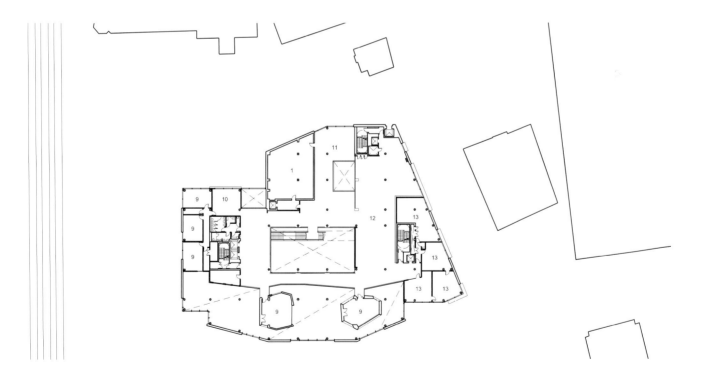

Second floor plan

SCALE
10m    20m    30m    40m    50m

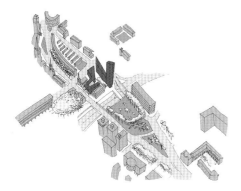

# BROADCASTING PLACE LEEDS METROPOLITAN UNIVERSITY

### OVERVIEW

Leeds Metropolitan University (LMU) was originally established as Leeds Polytechnic, an institution which evolved from the city's Technical College. During the late 1960s an enlarged campus was constructed on the northern edge of the city centre which reflected the city's contemporary ambition for modernisation and comprehensive redevelopment. It was an educational and architectural approach that introduced a revived artistic and design agenda to the city: an agenda that attracted my parents to move from London to take part in this new spirit. A generation later my parents still live in Leeds, and a fresh agenda has emerged for the new 'Leeds Met' University. A re-evaluation of the existing estate, in relation to contemporary/future educational agendas and pressures, has resulted in the university consolidating its existing stock while diversifying with a range of new locations throughout the city centre. Part of a generational shift, this sought to integrate the university into the city fabric as a series of interconnected facilities, creating a dynamic learning environment for the new millennium. The design of Broadcasting Place sought not only to deliver the requirements of the brief and respond to the history and context of the site but also to embody this transition to a more diverse and decentred urban university campus.

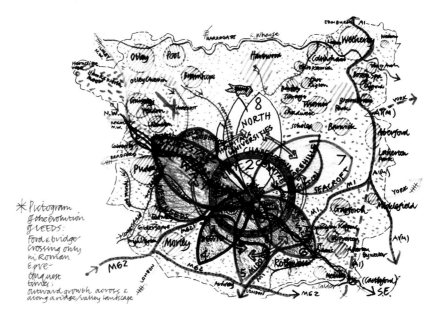

### RECONNECTING THE CITY

Located on a ridge overlooking the city centre, the site of Broadcasting Place marks a transition point between the commercial core, Leeds University campus and the inner city residential suburbs. This edge is marked by the Inner Ring Road which runs immediate to the site's southern boundary in a deep cutting, connected with associated slip roads and parking areas marking its route.

The work of the city's Civic Architect John Thorp for the Renaissance Project not only involved strategic masterplanning for the city core but also focused on strategies for reconnecting with what was termed as the city's 'inner rim'. While the

**opposite** Broadcasting Tower: South elevation towards the City Centre.

**top** Site context sketch in the context of the university quarter.

**bottom** Renaissance Leeds: A concept diagram of the city by John Thorp, Civic Architect.

**bottom** Barbara Hepworth, *The Family of Man*, Yorkshire Sculpture Park.

site's context to the south is more broken, its aspect to the north is the University Conservation Area with the key vista of Woodhouse Lane formed by Gothic church spires, grand brick terraces and terminated by the monolithic Portland stone tower of the Parkinson Building.

The site of Broadcasting Place housed the BBC Yorkshire headquarters and studios since the post-war period and the site had been effectively closed for a generation. Historically the site had previously housed the studio of Louis Le Prince, a French *émigré* whose 16 second film of a horse drawn carriage crossing Leeds Bridge is one of the first pieces of moving image.

## THE FLEXIBLE ACADEMIC SPACE

The brief for Broadcasting Place was outlined by Downing in conjunction with Leeds Met for the provision of academic accommodation, a new Baptist church to replace an outmoded one on the site and the provision of 240 student rooms. Downing would develop the site as a mixed-use scheme, providing a long lease to the university and, as such, accommodation was to be designed in a flexible enough manner for different users in the future. This flexibility allowed the university to decide the precise make-up of its own accommodation late into the design process. As such the design was progressed on the basis of a notional split between larger volume studio space and smaller scale administrative and communal teaching facilities, but without a specific breakdown. The Faculty of Arts and Humanities, as it eventually became, now houses Schools of Architecture, Landscape, Graphics, 3-D, Photography, Social Sciences and associated foyer, lecture, workshop and administrative support facilities. The overall area of the accommodation requirement reduced through discussions with the planners to 160,000 sq ft of academic floorspace along with Blenheim Baptist Church and 240 student rooms located in the Broadcasting Tower.

## AN ARCHITECTURAL LANDSCAPE

The conceptual design approach to the site evolved from the two-fold notion of a sculptural and landscape object that would be eroded and cut to create public space and architectural form. To the north of the city Brimham Rocks and the Craggs of Ilkley Moor provided inspiration for a weathered and rugged iconography rooted in its landscape context. These rock formations have inspired locally born sculptors Henry Moore and Barbara Hepworth and their abstraction of the elemental into sculpture and, in equal measure, inspired the development of the architecture of Broadcasting Place.

## THE ADAPTIVE OBJECT

Simple urban design moves carved key routes and spaces into the notional landscape form creating two separate building elements. Centred on a new open space, a series of routes through the site establish new and potential connections for the future—the main desire line being a new north–south pedestrian route linking the city centre with the inner suburbs. The sculptured mass of the buildings rise and fall around the site in order to respond to key frontages and respect the immediate and surrounding listed building context. The height and form of the building undulates and snakes around the site from its lowest level of three storeys along the main entrance frontage, rising to a mid-point of nine storeys before gently sloping to then abruptly rise to its dramatic peak at 23 storeys of the residential tower. The purity of this architectural approach is reinforced by maintaining a clean roofscape uninterrupted by plant, allowing the buildings to read more definitely as elements and allow them to integrate into the rising roof forms of the conservation area beyond.

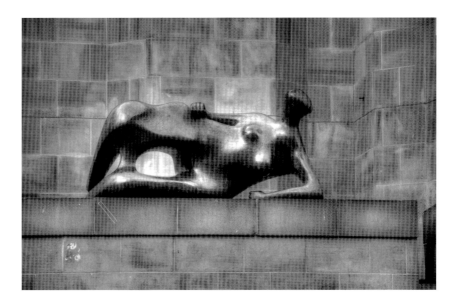

Separating the site into two buildings created a more administratively focused low-rise building which housed a generous reception and foyer with cafe/exhibition space relating directly to the main floors of flat floor teaching areas grouped around a covered external court. This central route creates an axis across the space to the entrance of the second building which accommodates the university's larger floor plate studio spaces. Each floor plate is split around a circulation core creating a smaller administration hub while the main area of the floor remains open and flexible studio space.

The orientation of the buildings is primarily north–south giving an east–west aspect to floors allowing for good general daylighting across floor plates. The studio block also runs parallel to the inner ring road slip roads and provides a good acoustic buffer to the centre of the site and the main public space. The site's location, raised on a ridge, allows for commanding views across the city centre and out to hills in the

top Henry Moore, *Reclining Figure*.

bottom Ground floor plan in the context of the urban motorways.

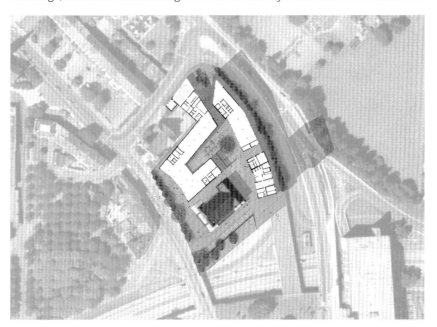

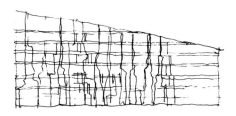

west and plains in the east. In particular on the upper levels, where the architectural and landscape studios are located, learning is always happening in relation to a link back to an experience of place. The intention of these visual connections between the studio environment and the urban environment will hopefully inform and enrich the experience of learning in the city.

The interiors of Broadcasting Place are set in marked contrast to the weathered quality of the exterior—employing a generally neutral backdrop with accent colours used to highlight circulation routes and help orientation. A concrete frame structure is expressed with exposed soffits, combining with lighting and servicing rafts in studio spaces and suspended ceilings to office areas. With an emphasis on lift circulation above first floor, the cores become a focal part of experiencing the building, giving access to lobby spaces that, in Block A in particular, allow for generous social learning spaces. The acoustic demands imposed by the adjacent road network were high but the building operates on a mixed mode ventilation system with opening lights, allowing for a more naturally ventilated approach as the roads become calmed over time.

### THE ABSTRACTED CLIFF

A simple palette of materials was chosen to unify all elements of the buildings: a material that was bold and would be identified with the university and would provide both a contrast and a complement to the white stone of the Parkinson Tower. There was also the desire to use a material that would work in the context of a predominantly brick backdrop and while being distinctive not be alien to its context. The use of a weathering steel draws influence from the sculptural intent behind the building and creates a material that changes according to elevation and aspect. In contrast, strong vertical slots articulate the overall weathered mass through slots of reflective glazing. These slots increase in width from the upper levels of the facade giving an impression of water flowing through rock—gradually weathering and eroding through the underlying strata.

### A RESPONSIVE FACADE

The elevations were configured through a full daylight mapping exercise that was undertaken with the Building Research Establishment. Each elevation was assessed to establish the optimum configuration of windows and areas of potential solar gain and overheating. This configuration was then refined to reflect the elevational composition. This was made more formal during the design process to create a base, middle and attic series of datum lines, to provide an order to otherwise informal elevations and give a scale and grain that allowed the building to fit more easily into its conservation area setting. Enlarged areas of glazing at ground and first floor levels provided a more generous public frontage to the scheme. These 'shop windows' place the foyer on open display, as well as the workshop, lecture rooms and Baptist Church itself. This also had the effect of removing the majority of steel from the ground plane, giving it both a perceived lightness and a flexibility for changes to other academic or commercial uses in the future. The most formal of these frontages is to the foyer on Woodhouse Lane where the inner concrete structure is exposed as a row of columns in a classically composed facade that responds to the porticoed frontages of the listed stone churches that flank it.

Broadcasting Tower houses two clusters of en-suite student rooms combined with larger accessible and studio rooms around a single core. Concierge and communal facilities are located at ground level where the entrance relates directly to the public realm,

**top** Concept sketches of studio elevation.

**bottom** Concept sketch of massing.

**opposite top** Concept sketch from the city looking towards the Leeds University building.

**opposite bottom** Massing model showing adjacency to highways and listed buildings.

fully integrating the residential and academic components of the scheme. The scale and location of the tower has intentionally become emblematic of the scheme as a whole and the sculpted, faceted and windowless facade that faces over the city centre has become a new landmark in Leeds.

In a city that has enjoyed a less adventurous form of commercial architecture during the recent development boom, Broadcasting Place was definitely a controversial building enjoying its fair share of criticism and praise. What the project did manage to achieve was to re-introduce an architectural dimension to the general debate within Leeds, placing the educational agenda and the university's profile firmly in the city's collective consciousness.

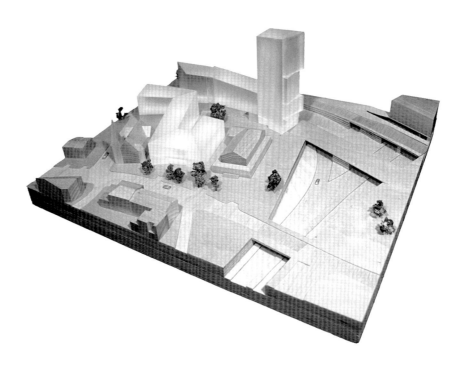

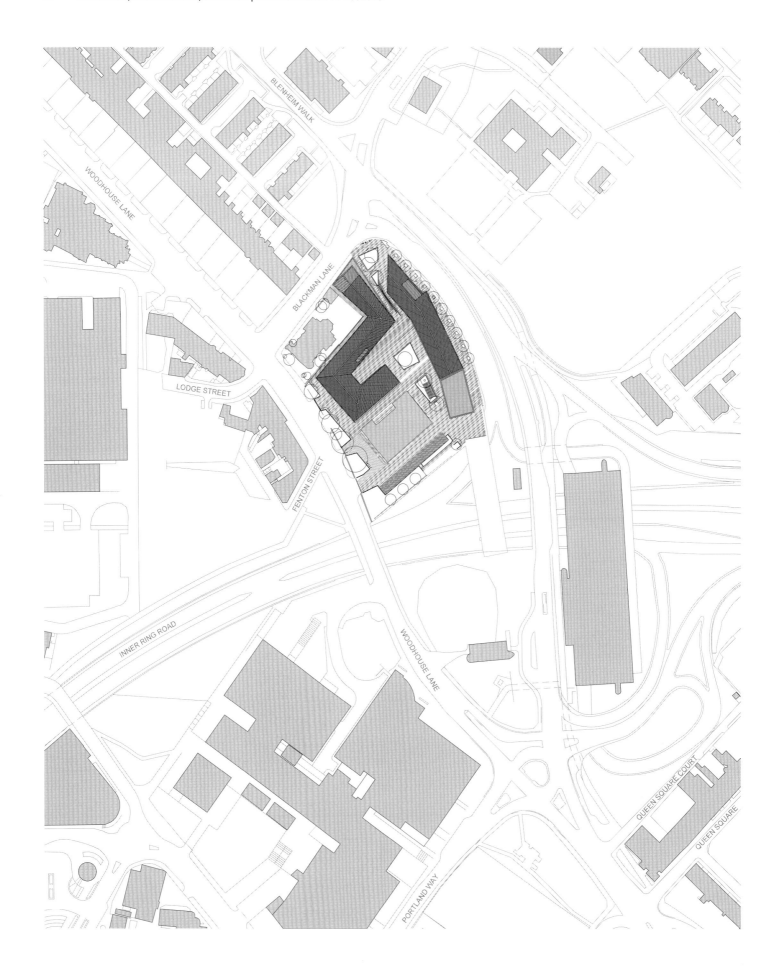

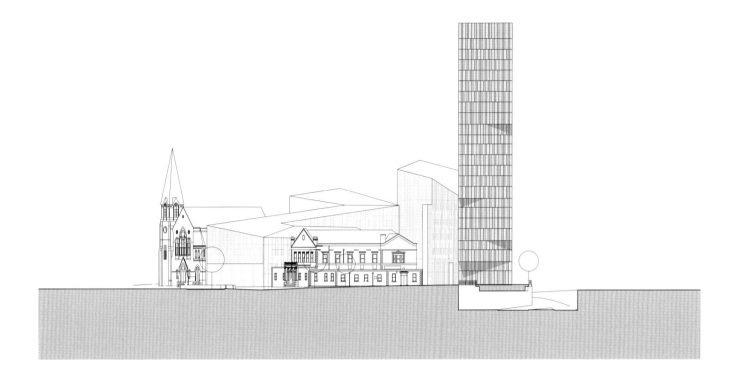

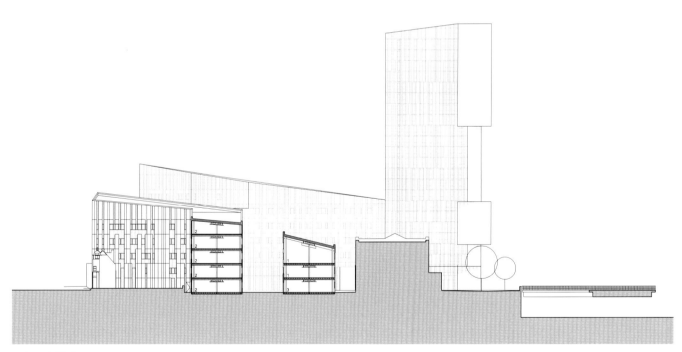

key  1. Staff area
     2. Teaching
     3. Exhibiton space

opposite  Site plan.
     top  Cross-section elevation A.
  bottom  Cross-section elevation B.

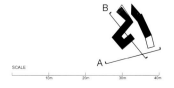

SCALE
10m      20m      30m      40m

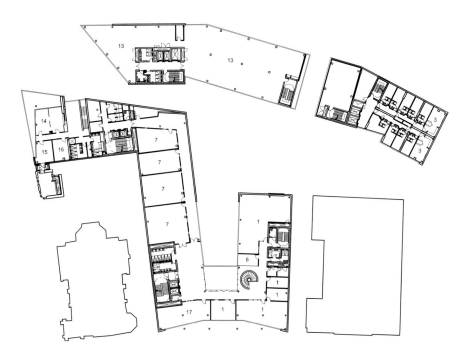

First floor plan

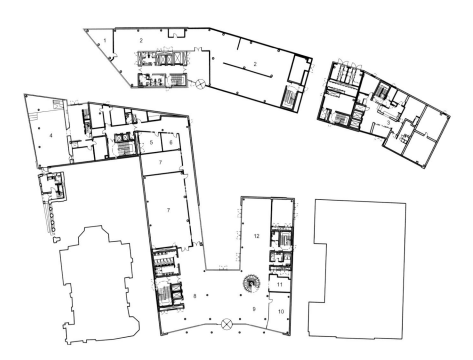

Ground floor plan

| key | 1. Staff Area | 6. Meeting room | 11. Cafe | 16. Church kitchen |
| --- | --- | --- | --- | --- |
| | 2. Workshop | 7. Teaching | 12. Exhibition space | 17. Research office |
| | 3. Student accommodation | 8. Helpzone | 13. Fine art workspace | 18. Contemporary practice workspace |
| | 4. Baptist church | 9. Reception | 14. Church meeting rooms | 19. Social learning area |
| | 5. Resource base | 10. Board room | 15. Creche | |

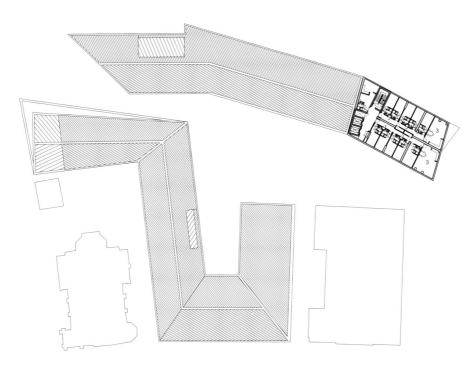

First floor plan

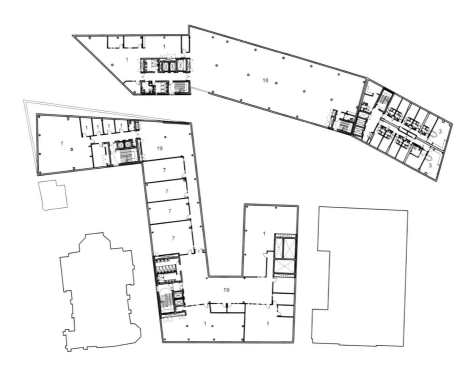

Ground floor plan

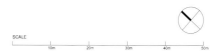

SCALE
10m          20m          30m          40m          50m

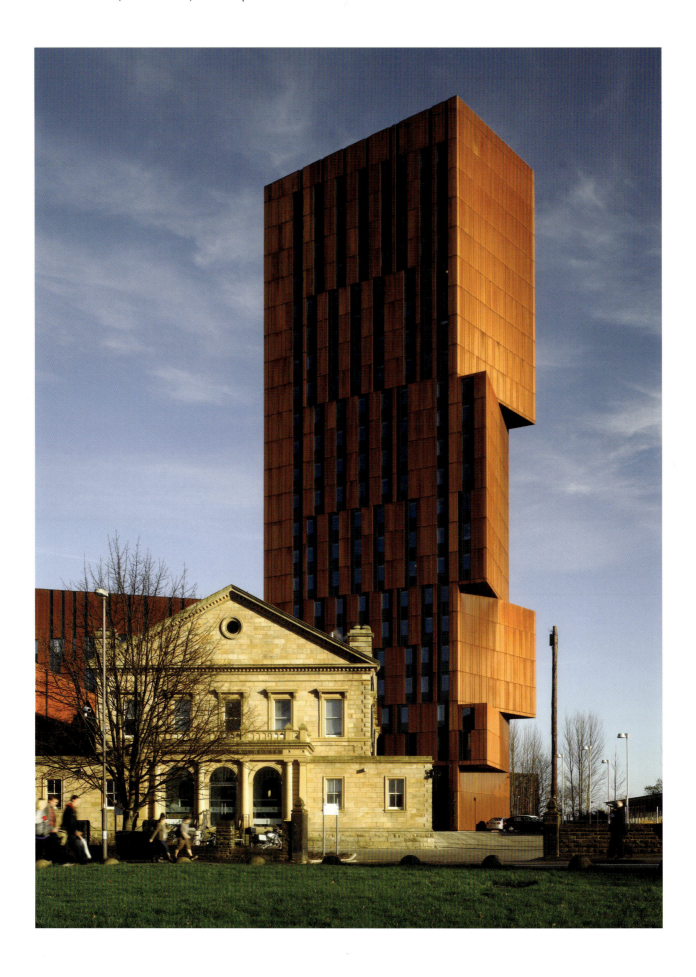

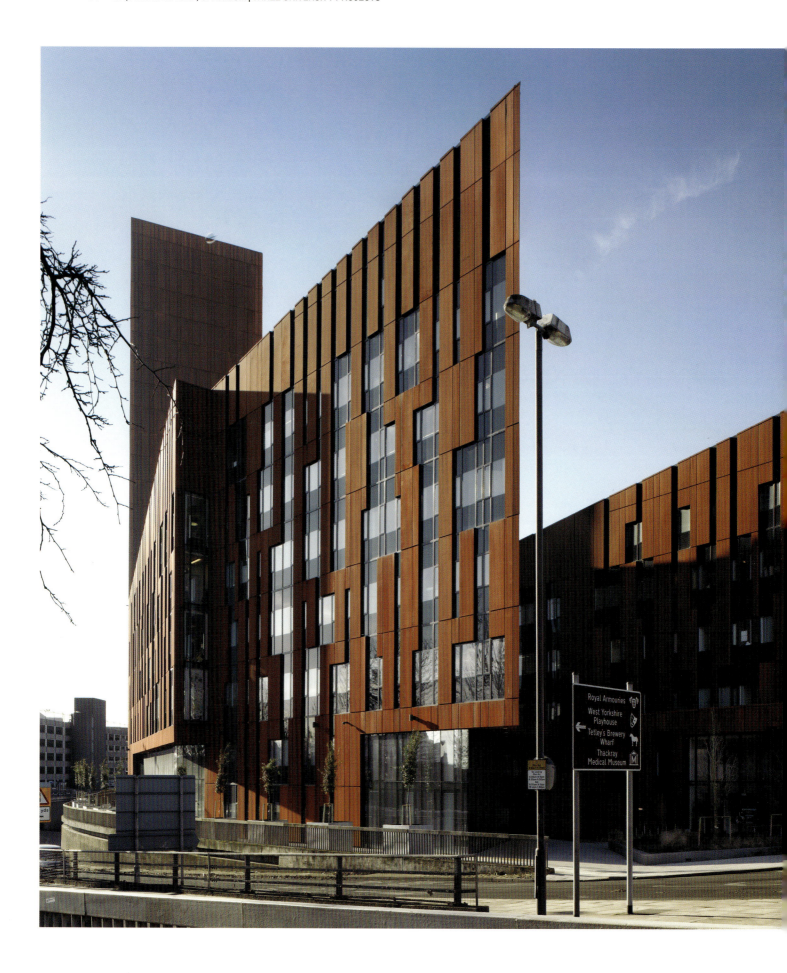

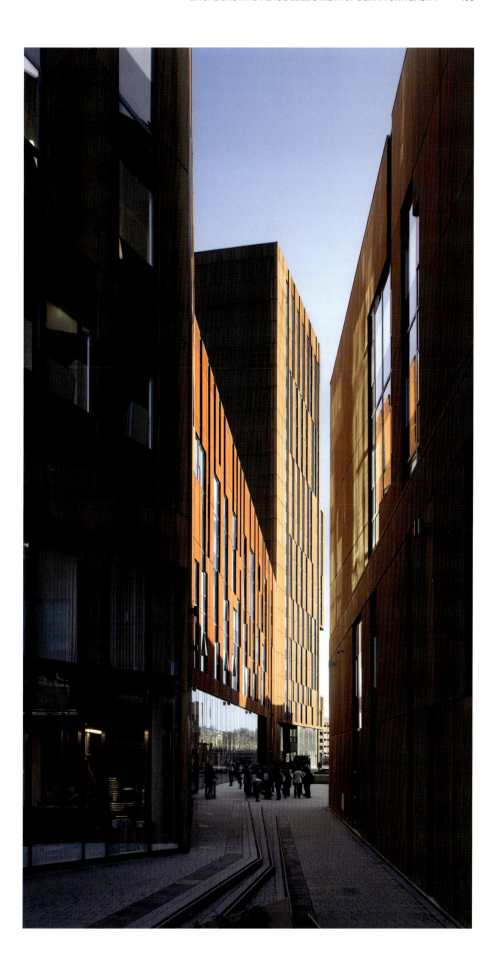

# CONCLUSION
# FURTHER THOUGHTS
# FROM ABROAD

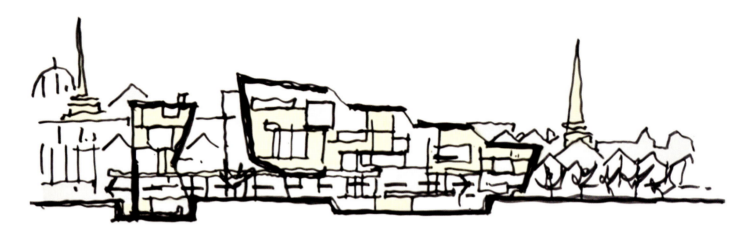

Universities have been around for about a thousand years but, just as in those graphs of energy consumption and population growth, we have seen exponential changes in the last two centuries. The graph below shows the increase in the numbers of universities in England from Oxford and Cambridge which can trace their ancestry back to the eleventh and twelfth centuries through to the expansion in the 'redbrick' universities of the nineteenth century and finally through three phases of expansion in the last 50 years. The first of these in the 1960s gave us the campus universities of York, Bath, Sussex, Surrey and many others that were detached from the cities that hosted them and were set up as ivory towers in green fields.

The second phase of growth, in 1992–1993, was in many cases a rebranding of older polytechnics, many of them with a history of a century or more—venerable institutions which tended to be more vocationally based but which saw their future as providing a broader-based academic education. The metropolitan universities of Leeds and Manchester fell into this category and the name they chose reflected their pride in their location at the heart of the cities they belonged to.

A final phase of change occurred in 2001–2002, granting university status to a series of smaller Colleges of Higher Education, which brought added status not only to the institutions but added social and economic value to the cities they served. The University of Worcester, growing out of a post-World War Two teacher training college was one of these, and the radical shift in status was seized upon to provide the integrated city/university library facility at the Hive.

1100    1200    1300    1400    1500

So what is the future of the university sector and, in particular, its potential role within urban regeneration? Significantly, in the decade from 2001 to 2011, despite the last four years of economic recession, undergraduate student numbers grew by 28 per cent and those enrolled in graduate courses grew a staggering 73 per cent. In February 2012, despite the fact that undergraduate applications from the UK and EU were down by 8.5 per cent and 11.5 per cent, applications from the rest of the world were up by 13.3 per cent and the income from foreign students continues to grow. So universities are practically the only sector of business that seems to have survived the recession without a downturn in income—though it remains to be seen whether swingeing cuts have a longer term effect on the quality of the education delivered.

Universities worldwide are becoming more cosmopolitan. Studying abroad is becoming a more sought after option in Higher Education, particularly if it results in acquiring new language skills but also an understanding of global culture. So universities are becoming cosmopolitan centres of learning, facilitating the exchange of culture, but also franchising their offer globally. One can only anticipate that cross-cultural collaboration will continue to grow, facilitated by internet connections and social networking but that, alongside this, the physical, social and cultural environment that host cities can provide will attract the best minds. Academic dialogue may well take place digitally, irrespective of location. Real meetings require real and rich environments that will only emerge from exercising our best skills in both architecture and urban design.

**opposite** Sectional sketch of the new University of Ulster Campus.

**bottom** The growth in numbers of universities in the United Kingdom. Dark blue indicates the incorporation with university status. Light blue indicates the date of foundation of preceding organisations.

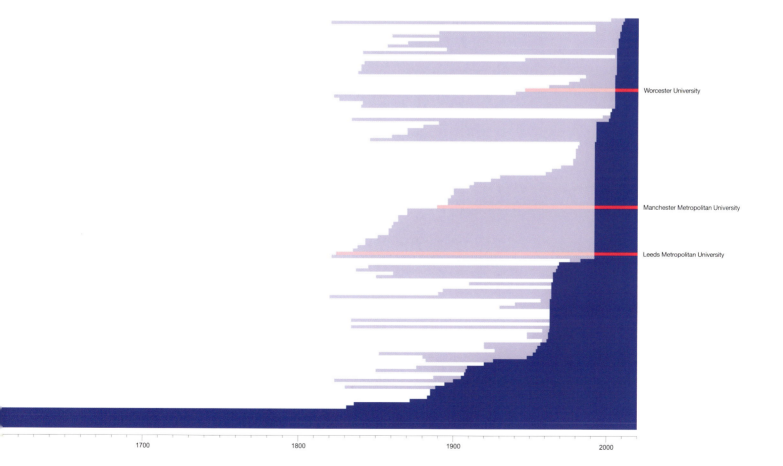

Worcester University

Manchester Metropolitan University

Leeds Metropolitan University

1700          1800          1900          2000

top Principal elevations of the new University of Ulster Campus in the centre of the city.

opposite top Sectional diagram of the new University of Ulster Campus.

opposite centre Integrated Planning and Design Facility, University of British Columbia, Vancouver.

opposite bottom Integration of landscape and sustainability strategies.

Our ventures overseas have upheld this thinking. In 2010 we won a competition to relocate the University of Ulster from Jordanstown on the edge of Belfast, where it had been built as part of the first round of expansion mentioned above, back into the heart of the city. Here, sacrificing suburban space for urban vitality, and recognising that the city needs the university as much as the university needs the city, we are building a multi-level campus that brings together different departments under one roof, or at least in a series of interlinked buildings. Externally the building complex will be as much a statement of regeneration of the city as of the acceptance of a new role for the university as a driver of social and economic change in an urban environment that has long suffered from poverty and sectarianism. Internally it is organised around those principles of holistic learning, which mean that the buildings are there to provide spaces to study, learn and listen, as well as relax, talk, eat and drink.

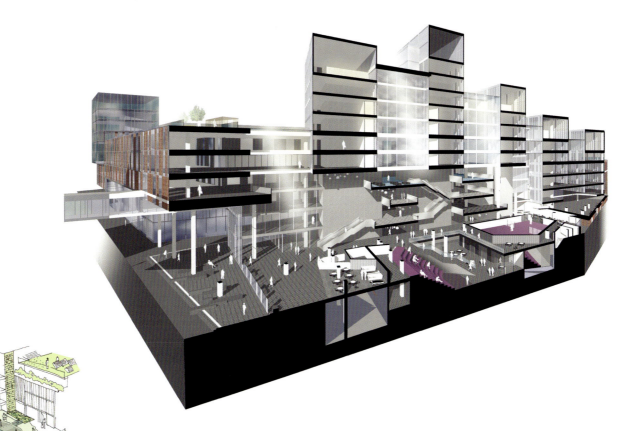

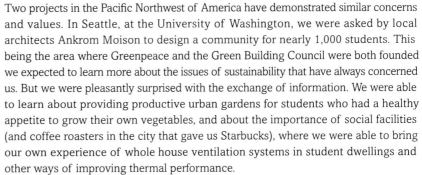

Two projects in the Pacific Northwest of America have demonstrated similar concerns and values. In Seattle, at the University of Washington, we were asked by local architects Ankrom Moison to design a community for nearly 1,000 students. This being the area where Greenpeace and the Green Building Council were both founded we expected to learn more about the issues of sustainability that have always concerned us. But we were pleasantly surprised with the exchange of information. We were able to learn about providing productive urban gardens for students who had a healthy appetite to grow their own vegetables, and about the importance of social facilities (and coffee roasters in the city that gave us Starbucks), where we were able to bring our own experience of whole house ventilation systems in student dwellings and other ways of improving thermal performance.

Similarly in Vancouver, working with Shape Architecture on a new extension to the School of Architecture to produce an Integrated Planning and Design faculty, we found the same concerns over producing a range of interior and exterior spaces that allowed flexibility of use, encouraged interdiscipliniarity, and made connections between the man-made and the natural world that symbolised the ambitions of the School of Landscape and Architecture. Both of these projects have been learning vehicles for ourselves as well as our collaborators.

So if the future of universities locally is in creating buildings and urban spaces which are more closely integrated with their host cities, the future of universities globally is in cross-cultural collaboration in teaching and in research. Education may not require architecture or urbanism to fulfill the basic requirement of the acquisition and interpretation of knowledge. But high quality architecture and urbanism will generate the environment for academic minds to flourish and for the vital social element of education to thrive.

# CONTRIBUTOR BIOGRAPHIES

## PROFESSOR JEREMY TILL

Head, Central Saint Martins College of Arts and Design
Pro Vice-Chancellor, University of the Arts London

Professor Jeremy Till became Head of Central Saint Martins and Pro Vice-Chancellor of the University of Arts London in August 2012. As Head of College, leading one of the world's most celebrated centres for creative education and research, he holds responsibility for Central Saint Martins' 4,500 students and 400 staff, and the further development of its tradition of experimentation, innovation and risk-taking.

Prior to this he was Executive Dean of the School of Architecture and the Built Environment at the University of Westminster and, before that, he was Professor and Head of the School of Architecture at the University of Sheffield from 1999 to 2008. He has also held roles at the Bartlett School of Architecture (University College London), the University of Pennsylvania and Kingston University.

## PROFESSOR JOHN BROOKS

Vice Chancellor,
Manchester Metropolitan University

Professor John Brooks was appointed Vice-Chancellor of Manchester Metropolitan University in September 2005 from his previous position as Vice Chancellor of the University of Wolverhampton. A physics graduate of the University of Sheffield, John Brooks was awarded a DSc in 1998 for his work in the physics of materials which spanned some 25 years and resulted in three patents that enabled him to set up a joint venture company.

Nationally, he has served as Chair of the Equality Challenge Unit and as a member of the Board of Universities UK. Currently, he is Deputy Chair of the Board of the Universities and Colleges Employers Association (UCEA) and sits on several national committees.

At regional level, he has served on th.e Board of the Northwest Development Agency. He is the new Chair of Corridor Manchester, a collaboration between the two Manchester Universities, the City Council and the Manchester Royal Infirmary,
which develops and extends the knowledge capacity to serve the city's social, community and economic ambitions. Professor Brooks has a particular interest in the development of vocational education and the improvement of educational opportunities at all levels, and strongly supports the increase in participation and widening access, believing that Higher Education should be available to all who can benefit from it.

He is currently leading on a £350 million investment programme in new teaching and learning facilities as the university undergoes the largest physical change to its estate since its foundation and consolidates from seven to two campuses.

## ANDREW HARRISON

Managing Director,
Spaces That Work Ltd

Andrew Harrison founded Spaces That Work Ltd in 2010. An international independent design consultancy firm, Spaces That Work Ltd focuses on the creation of innovative and effective educational environments. Andrew undertakes educational research and design projects in schools and universities and has published widely on learning spaces, intelligent buildings and the future workplace.

Prior to this Andrew was a Director of DEGW plc. He was responsible for the development of DEGW's learning environments work globally and leader of the UK learning team, and undertook a wide range of research and consultancy projects both in the UK and internationally.

He is currently Deputy Chair and Trustee of the Crafts Council and also Chair of Global Yell, a Shetland-based arts development charity focusing on music and textiles.

## KEITH BRADLEY

Senior Partner,
Feilden Clegg Bradley Studios

Keith Bradley is a Senior Partner with Feilden Clegg Bradley Studios (FCBS), based in London and Bath. He joined the practice in 1987, was made a partner in 1995 and, in 1998, he set up the London office. Keith is a Chair of the Design Council CABE National and London Design Review.

Keith has led numerous FCBS award-winning projects that have included 30 RIBA Awards, the Queen's Award for Sustainability and the 2008 RIBA Stirling Prize. Keith has led the design of award-winning high-density urban regeneration schemes throughout the UK including the 2008 Stirling Prize winning Accordia housing development in Cambridge, UK. His public buildings portfolio includes a number of UK university commissions including buildings for Imperial College; Queen Mary College; UCL and studies for the London School of Economics. The new Business School and Student Hub for Manchester Metropolitan University has been recently completed with the new School of Art and Design on site. Keith is also currently leading the design for the major new £170 million city centre urban campus for the University of Ulster in Belfast.

Keith is a guest critic and lecturer at numerous Schools of Architecture in the UK and a frequent speaker at conferences in the UK and abroad, particularly on urban regeneration and architecture for education.

## PROFESSOR PETER CLEGG

Founding Partner,
Feilden Clegg Bradley Studios

Professor Peter Clegg is a Founding Partner with Feilden Clegg Bradley Studios, having established the practice with Richard Feilden in 1978. Widely regarded as a pioneer in the field of environmental design, he has more than 30 years' experience in low energy architecture and is actively involved in research, design and education.

Peter was the primary author of *Feilden Clegg Bradley: The Environmental Handbook*, published in 2007, a substantial account of the practice's sustainable design experience over the last 30 years.

Peter was Senior Partner in charge of the architectural developments at the Yorkshire Sculpture Park and the new Central Office for the National Trust in Swindon. Recently completed university projects include the Higher Education scheme at Broadcasting Place for Leeds Metropolitan University. Recent work abroad includes the Leventis Art Gallery in Cyprus, a new school for the Aga Khan Foundation in Kyrgystan, a new school of architecture and planning at the University of British Columbia, and a 900 bed student housing scheme for the University of Seattle.

He is Chair of the CABE affiliated South West Design Review Panel and a Trustee of the Yorkshire Sculpture Park and was made a Royal Designer for Industry (RDI) in 2010.

## SIMON DOODY

Partner,
Feilden Clegg Bradley Studios

Simon Doody joined Feilden Clegg Bradley Studios' Bath office in 2003 was made a Partner in 2007.

Since joining FCBS, Simon has developed an expertise in the education sector, first working on a DfES-commissioned exemplar design for an All Age Community School, or 'Through School'. He then lead the design for a new City Academy in Paddington and, most recently, has been overseeing the design of the new Business School and Student Hub for Manchester Metropolitan University. He has written about the pedagogical and pastoral approaches to education design in a number of publications.

He has recently been appointed to lead the work on a new student union project for Manchester Metropolitan University as well as acting as a consultant for the refurbishment of the main library.

## JO WRIGHT

Partner Studio Leader,
Feilden Clegg Bradley Studios

Jo Wright joined Feilden Clegg Bradley Studios in 1989 and became a Partner in 1995. Jo has been responsible for the design and delivery of a wide range of award-winning buildings including highly sustainable headquarters for the National Trust, the Woodland Trust and Greenpeace and projects at the Universities of Winchester, Southampton, Birmingham, Aston and Bath.

Recently-completed projects include the Hive, the UK's first joint-use library for the University of Worcester which is the first FCBS project to achieve BREEAM 'outstanding', the Dyson Centre for Neonatal Care at the Royal United Hospital in Bath and the practice's first hotel, the Magdalen Chapter in Exeter.

Current projects include an art gallery and luxury apartments in Nicosia, Cyprus and the University of Bath's Centre for the Arts.

## ALEX WHITBREAD

Partner,
Feilden Clegg Bradley Studios

Alex Whitbread joined Feilden Clegg Bradley Studios' London office in 1998 and was made a Partner in 2007. Alex works across a range of projects in the practice, focusing on urban design and large-scale city centre buildings.

Alex has worked on a number of major regeneration projects in the UK, particularly in the north in Manchester and Leeds, including the multi-award winning Broadcasting Place project for Leeds Metropolitan University.

He is currently Project Leader for Nine Elms, the masterplan and design of a large residential and mixed-use project adjacent to the new American Embassy in London; South Lambeth Road student residential tower in Vauxhall; Highfield Humanities College in Blackpool; Globe Road Residential Scheme in Holbeck, Leeds, and is leading the design for the University of Ulster Greater Belfast Development from the London office.

# EDUCATION ARCHITECTURE URBANISM PROJECT CREDITS

## MANCHESTER METROPOLITAN UNIVERSITY BUSINESS SCHOOL AND STUDENT HUB

| | |
|---|---|
| Keith Bradley | Senior Partner in charge |
| David Stansfield | Studio Leader/Partner |
| Simon Doody | Project Architect/Partner |
| Alex Morris | Architect |
| Michael Woodford | Architect |
| Martin Hedges | Architect |
| Kristof Gomory | Architect |
| Sara Haghshenass | Architectural Assistant |
| Filippo Girotti | Architectural Assistant |
| Matthew Sommerville | Architect |
| Louise Wray | Architect |
| John Moran | Architect |
| Ken Grix | Model-maker/Partner |

**CLIENT** Manchester Metropolitan University

**PROJECT MANAGER** Manchester Metropolitan University

**STRUCTURAL ENGINEER** White Young Green

**M&E ENGINEER** AECOM

**COST CONSULTANT** Rider Levett Bucknall

**CONTRACTOR** Sir Robert McAlpine

**CDM COORDINATOR** Appleyard and Trew

**FACADE CONSULTANT** Montresor Partnership

**LANDSCAPE** PlanitIE

## THE HIVE
## UNIVERSITY OF WORCESTER

| | |
|---|---|
| Jo Wright | Studio Leader/Partner |
| Matt Vaudin | Architect/Partner (bid) |
| Andy Couling | Architect/Partner (delivery) |
| Iain Williams | Project Architect |
| Richard Priest | Generative Designer |
| Laszlo Balazs | Architect |
| Nick Hodges | Architect |
| Kirsten Williams | Architect |
| Charlotte Knight | Architectural Assistant |
| Holly Gilleland | Project Administrator |
| Hester Brough | Architect |
| Tim Healy | Architect |
| Matthew Morrish | Architect |
| Matt Williams | Architect |
| Tom Foggin | Architectural Assistant |
| Will Laslett | Architectural Assistant |
| Nathan Ovens | Architectural Assistant |
| Ken Grix | Model-maker/Partner |
| Matt Rees | 3DCreate, model-maker |
| Toby Lewis | Consultant |
| David Saxby | 00:/, bid consultant |

**CLIENT** University of Worcester and Worcestershire County Council

**STRUCTURAL ENGINEER** Hyder Consulting (UK) Ltd/Atelier One

**M&E ENGINEER** Max Fordham LLP

**CDM COORDINATOR** Arcadis AYH

**LANDSCAPE CONSULTANT** Grant Associates

**CONTRACTOR** Galliford Try Construction

**CLADDING CONSULTANT** Montresor Partnership

**FIRE CONSULTANT** Exova Warringtonfire

**ACCESS CONSULTANT** All Clear Designs

## BROADCASTING PLACE
## LEEDS METROPOLITAN UNIVERSITY

| | |
|---|---|
| Peter Clegg | Senior Partner in charge |
| Julian Gitsham | Managing Partner |
| Alex Whitbread | Architect/Partner |
| Simon Carter | Project Architect |
| Oliver Kampshoff | Architect |
| Marta Ferre | Architect |
| Andrew Macintosh | Architect |
| Alexandra Machado | Architect |
| Rud Sawers | Architect |
| Richard Priest | Generative Designer |
| Mellis Haward | Architectural Assistant |
| Michael Riebel | Architectural Assistant |
| Ruth Kedar | Architectural Assistant |
| Neil Sansom | Architectural Assistant |
| Mike Luszczak | Concept Design |

**CLIENT** Downing and Leeds Metropolitan University

**STRUCTURAL ENGINEER** Halcrow Yolles

**EMPLOYER'S AGENT** Ridge and Partners LLP

**LANDSCAPE ARCHITECT** Robert Myers Associates

**MAIN CONTRACTOR** George Downing Construction

**SERVICES ENGINEER** KGA Trinity Chamber

**FACADE CONSULTANT** Montresor Partnership

**PLANNING CONSULTANT** Matthew & Goodman

## THREE UNIVERSITY PROJECTS
## COPYRIGHT LIST CREDIT

©Hufton+Crow/pp. 26 (t), 38, 50, 51, 52, 53, 54, 55, 56, 57, 58, 59, 60, 61, 62, 72, 73, 74, 75, 76, 77, 78, 79, 80, 81, 82, 83, 84, 85, 86, 87.

©Will Pryce/pp. 21(b), 88, 98, 99, 100, 101, 102, 103, 104, 105, 106, 107, 108, 109, 110, 111, 112, 113.

©Simon Kirwan/pp. 9, 36, 37.

©by kind permission of the Master and Fellows of Trinity College/p. 19.

©Reinhard Görner/p. 20 (t).

©Kevin Allen/p. 20 (b).

©Daniel Hopkinson/p. 28 (l).

©Max Fordham LLP/p. 31 (tr).

©Manchester Libraries, Information and Archives, Manchester City Council/p. 39 (b)

©John Thorp/p. 89 (b).

©Therasa Blemings 2012/p. 90(t).

©Nigel Homer/pp. 90 (b).

©James Meehan/pp. 91(t).

© AVR London/pp. 116, 117(t).

© SHAPE Architecture Inc/pp. 117(c, b).

All other images are © Feilden Clegg Bradley Studios.

## SPONSORSHIP
## MANCHESTER METROPOLITAN UNIVERSITY

Manchester Metropolitan University is one of the largest, most diverse and most popular UK universities. The estates consolidation programme, with a spend of some £350 million over a nine year period, has helped to redefine the relationship between the full fee-paying student and the university. www.mmu.ac.uk

### Sir Robert McAlpine

Sir Robert McAlpine Limited is a leading UK building and civil engineering company founded in 1869. Family-owned and with a reputation for innovation and quality, the company's pioneering approach to construction and commitment to service has ensured its continued presence at the forefront of the industry. www.sir-robert-mcalpine.com

### Downing

"The provision of high quality educational facilities incorporating student accommodation is increasingly recognised as a key marketing factor in Higher Education. In order to meet enrollment targets, universities and colleges need to offer high quality accommodation that reflects well on the education brand. At Downing, we are proud to be a pioneer of world class, sustainable buildings for education. We understand only too well the importance of student accommodation schemes and work with universities, award-winning architects and project teams to ensure our projects provide a sense of place in their urban context." George Downing. www.downing.com

### Grant Associates

Grant Associates is a landscape architecture consultancy specialising in the creative design of both urban and rural environments. The consultancy is involved in a number of forward-looking projects throughout the UK, Europe and the Far East, often working with some of the world's leading architects and designers. www.grant-associates.uk.com

### PlanitIE

PlanitIE are landscape architects and urban designers. A creative studio which values healthy, sustainable places to live, work, and play. PlanitIE has collaborated with clients, architects and engineers, artists and craftspeople on a wide range of projects in the UK and internationally. www.planit-ie.com

## ACKNOWLEDGMENTS

Like all of our design work the making of this book has involved a dedicated team which in this case brought together key representatives of the architectural teams for each building. For Feilden Clegg Bradley Studios the production of the book has been led by Simon Doody. We are grateful to Matt Barrass for producing all the drawings. But we are truly indebted to Fliss Childs for managing the process, coordinating text, drawings and captions, liaising with our colleagues at Artifice, and chasing us all on a regular basis!

Artifice books on architecture
10a Acton Street
London WC1X 9NG
United Kingdom

Tel: +44 (0)20 7713 5097
Fax: +44 (0)20 7713 8682
sales@artificebooksonline.com
www.artificebooksonline.com

All opinions expressed within this publication are those of the authors and not necessarily of the publisher.

British Library Cataloguing-in-Publication Data. A CIP record for this book is available from the British Library.

ISBN 978 1 908967 04 6

Designed by Rachel Pfleger at Artifice books on architecture.

Artifice books on architecture is an environmentally responsible company. *Education Architecture Urbanism: Three University Projects* is printed on sustainably sourced paper.